DIALOGUES ON THE PSYCHOLOGY OF LANGUAGE AND THOUGHT

Conversations with

Noam Chomsky
Charles Osgood
Jean Piaget
Ulric Neisser *and*
Marcel Kinsbourne

COGNITION AND LANGUAGE
A Series in Psycholinguistics
Series Editor: R. W. RIEBER

CLINICAL PSYCHOLINGUISTICS
Theodore Shapiro

CRAZY TALK: A Study of the Discourse of Schizophrenic Speakers
Sherry Rochester and J. R. Martin

PSYCHOLOGY OF LANGUAGE AND LEARNING
O. Hobart Mowrer

DIALOGUES ON THE PSYCHOLOGY OF LANGUAGE AND THOUGHT
Edited by Robert W. Rieber

A Continuation Order Plan is available for this series. A continuation order will bring delivery of each new volume immediately upon publication. Volumes are billed only upon actual shipment. For further information please contact the publisher.

DIALOGUES ON THE PSYCHOLOGY OF LANGUAGE AND THOUGHT

Conversations with
Noam Chomsky
Charles Osgood
Jean Piaget
Ulric Neisser and
Marcel Kinsbourne

Edited by
ROBERT W. RIEBER
*City University of New York
and Columbia University
College of Physicians and Surgeons
New York, New York*

in collaboration with GILBERT VOYAT
*City College and the Graduate Center, CUNY
New York, New York*

PLENUM PRESS • NEW YORK AND LONDON

Library of Congress Cataloging in Publication data

Main entry under title:

Dialogues on the psychology of language and thought.

(Cognition and language)
Bibliography: p.
Includes index.
1. Psycholinguistics—Addresses, essays, lectures. 2. Thought and thinking—Addresses, essays, lectures. I. Chomsky, Noam. II. Rieber, R. W. (Robert W.) III. Voyat, Gilbert. IV. Series.

P37.D52 1983   401'.9   82-42850
ISBN 0-306-41185-7

© 1983 Plenum Press, New York
A Division of Plenum Publishing Corporation
233 Spring Street, New York, N.Y. 10013

Printed in the United States of America

Preface

The scope and variety of interest areas identified with psycholinguistic research have grown enormously during the last decade or two. Although this recent flourishing has brought a great deal of new knowledge and interdisciplinary cooperation to the field, it has also brought its share of controversy and confusion as conflicting views on a number of important topics are hotly debated by their proponents. It is for this reason that we have put together this book, a collection of interviews with a number of leading scholars within the field, all of whom differ--sometimes widely-- in their respective points of view.

The idea of using a uniform set of questions as points of departure for each interview seemed to us a choice method for providing readers with a better understanding of the complexities of the field. The questions we have chosen to work with are crucial questions for psycholinguistics since they form the framework for knowledge and research within the field. It is our hope that by offering several different points of view on psycholinguistic research, this volume will provide readers with a better sense of the similarities and differences of opinion within these different points of view.

We would like to extend our thanks to the various contributors to this book for their cooperation and patience during the preparation of this book, and to the publishers for their steady encouragement during our work.

November 1, 1982   R.W. Rieber

Contents

PART I

INTRODUCTION

INTRODUCTION

An Overview of the Controversial Issues in the Psychology of Language and Thought

R. W. RIEBER AND GILBERT VOYAT

4

Professor of Psychology at John Jay College of Criminal Justice and also on the faculty of the Psychiatry Department, Columbia University, College of Physicians and Surgeons.

Dr. Rieber is founder and editor of the Journal of Communication Disorders as well as the Journal of Psycholinguistic Research. A list of some of his publications are as follows:

With R.S. Brubaker, eds., Speech Pathology, 1966, North-Holland; The Neuropsychology of Language, ed., Plenum Publishing Corporation, 1976; The Problem of Stuttering: Theory and Therapy, ed., North-Holland, 1977; with R. Aaronson, eds., Developmental Psycholinguistics and Communication Disorders, New York Academy of Science, 1975; with Kurt Salzinger, eds., The Roots of American Psychology, 1977; Language Development and Aphasia in Children, ed., Academic Press, in press; Psychology of Language and Thought, ed., Plenum Publishing Corporation, 1980; Body and Mind, ed., Academic Press, 1980; Psychological Foundations of Criminal Justice with Harold Vetter, John Jay Press, 1978, plus many articles in scientific journals.

Dr. Rieber has taught at Rutgers University and Pace University, received his B.S. from Pennsylvania State University, Masters degree from Temple University and his Ph.D. from University College of University of London. He is a fellow of the New York Academy of Sciences, fellow of the American Association for the Advancement of Science and the American Anthropological Association.

Dr. Robert W. Rieber
10 East 85th Street
New York, New York 10028

Gilbert E. Voyat is Professor of Psychology at the City College and the Graduate Center of the City University of New York, where he is associated with Graduate Programs in clinical, experimental-cognition and developmental psychology. He was born in Bienne (Switzerland), took his Ph.D. under Prof. Jean Piaget's direction at the University of Geneva. He was a student, research associate and instructor for several years at the International Center for Genetic Epistemology at the Faculty of Science at the University of Geneva. His research includes psychopathology the field of genetic epistemology, identity, mental imagery, memory and perception.

He came in 1966 to the United States at the request of the Massachussetts Institute of Technology (MIT) where he did research in the field of artificial intelligence. Between 1968 and 1972 he was Assistant then Associate Professor at Yeshiva University and he is presently Professor of Clinical Psychology at the City University of New York.

In this country he has been affiliated with the Office of Health, Education and Welfare (HEW) in the Indian Health Service in the Department of Mental Health. In this connection he has conducted various comparative studies and workshops among Indian teachers and children, Sioux in South Dakota and Navaho Indians in Arizona and New Mexico.

He is currently doing research sponsored by the Department of Health Education and Welfare (HEW) with autistic children.

He has also directed several missions for the United Nations Developmental Program (UNDP) in West Africa and Asia.

His work includes: I.Q., God given or man-made? Saturday Review, Vol. 52 May 17, 1969. The development of operations: a theoretical and practical question, Chap. 7 in Piaget in the Classroom, edited by M. Schwebel and J. Rap, Basic Books, New York, 1973. Perception and concept of time, Chap. 4 in The Personal Experience of Time, edited by B. S. Gorman and A. E. Wessman, Plenum Press, London and New York, 1977. Tribute to Piaget: A look at his scientific impact in the United States, Part VI, Chap. 3 in The Roots of American Psychology: Historical Influences and Implications for the Future, edited by R. W. Rieber and K. Salzinger, Annals of the New York Academy of Sciences, Vol. 291, 1977. Piaget on schizophrenia, Journal of the American Academy of Psychoanalysis, Vol. 8, No. 1. 93-113, 1980. Piaget Systematized, Larry Erlbaum Associates, New Jersey, 1981.

An Overview of the Controversial Issues on the Psychology of Language and Thought

R. W. Rieber and G. Voyat
City University of New York

This book presents the reader with a combination of two levels of interaction. The first involves the relationship between the mind and language, and the second the relationship of two individuals communicating in a dialogue. The combination of both of these features in one book is unique to the scientific literature in this field.

Unusual also is the use of a uniform set of questions as points of departure for each dialogue. The seven questions chosen to constitute the body of this work provide the reader, in the form of a dialogue, answers to some of the most important contemporary issues in the field of psychology of language and thought. Although they cover a wide range of issues, they are not intended to evoke a comprehensive survey of the field. Rather, they are intended to touch seminal points of controversy, making the viewpoints of leading authorities available to both students and scholars.

The seven questions listed below were circulated to all of the individuals interviewed in this book before the dialogues were transcribed. All of the authors agreed that these questions would constitute a useful basis and structure for the dialogue.

The seven questions are as follows:-

1. What role does cognition play in the acquisition and the development of language? Do linguistic factors influence general cognitive development?

7

2. How is the acquisition and development of language influenced
    by interpersonal and intrapersonal verbal and nonverbal behavior?

3. Are the verbal and nonverbal signal systems interrelated?

4. How can one best deal with the issue of nature versus nurture
    in our attempts to unravel the basic issues in the field of
    language and cognition?

    a. Of what importance is the biological basis of language
        perception and production?

    b. Of what importance is the study of individuals who suffer
        from pathological conditions of language and thought?

5. Of what importance is the current research in comparative
    psycholinguistics (recent attempts to train chimpanzees and/or
    apes via sign language or any other method)?

6. What are the most important and promising applications of
    research in the psychology of language and cognition?

7. Do you feel that the field of language and cognition is, as
    some believe, in a state of transition searching for a new
    theory or paradigm? If so, what kind of theory do you believe
    will emerge or is at present emerging?

QUESTION 1

    Our first dialogue was with Noam Chomsky. Chomsky begins by
rewording the first question to ask "what role other aspects of
cognition play in the acquisition and development of language."
Rather than viewing cognition and language as separate but interacting factors, he views language as "one aspect of cognition and
its development as one aspect of the development of cognition." He
views cognition itself as being composed of many specific and distinct cognitive systems. These cognitive systems have unique
properties, peculiarities, and modes of action. They are specifically structured and highly articulated, and genetically determined
by their basic outline. Language is considered to be one of these
systems. To clarify the theory that cognitive systems are composed
of separate structures, Chomsky provides an analogy with the development of human organs and systems (i.e. the circulatory system,
reproductive system, liver, kidney.) Elaborating upon this analogy,
Chomsky states that just as the scientist can observe the maturation

of physical organs, so too, he can trace the development of mental
organs of specific mental capacities. He describes this scientific
process as follows:

> "Language is simply one of these (mental) structures.....I'm
> sure if we were to study, to take another distinctly human
> characteristic, our capacity to deal with properties of the
> number system — it's unique to humans, as far as we know, a
> specific capacity of the human mind — one might, for example,
> try to explore the properties of that system in a mature
> person. We might then ask how that system develops through
> childhood, what kind of stimulation from the environment is
> necessary for it to develop to its mature state, and so on.
> In doing so we would have studied the growth of a particular
> mental organ to its mature state.....The language system can
> be, and, in fact, is being studied in essentially this way.
> Similarly, we could study the other mental organs.....In this
> way we could develop what seems to me a reasonable version of
> 'faculty psychology'."

Chomsky goes on to define several important concepts. He views
cognition as an aspect of our belief, knowledge or understanding.
Moreover, he views language as one of many systems that interact to
form the complex of interconnected cognitive structures.

From the extreme rationalist position in our first dialogue
with linguist Noam Chomsky, we now encounter a more empiricist position stressed by psychologist Charles Osgood.

Osgood expresses his belief that cognizing (which involves the
abilities to comprehend and react to perceived events or states) is
developed in pre-linguistic prior to linguistic processing, both in
the species and the developing child. Such pre-linguistic processing
dominates in the first two or three years of life, and then tapers
off while still influencing the development of linguistic processing.
Additionally, since cognitive structures are primarily based on pre-
linguistic experiences, and since there is a strong relationship .
between language development and pre-linguistic cognizing, Osgood
emphasizes the significant role that perceptual cognizing plays in
language development.

Osgood thus relates development of the structuring of simplex
sentences to the basic fundamentals of pre-linguistic cognizing.
As stated in his "Naturalness Principle", he feels that the more the
surface structures of sentences correspond to the pre-linguistically
determined cognitive structures, the earlier such sentences will
appear in development and, additionally, the more easily they will
be processed by adults.

In the second part of the first question Osgood mentions the influence of linguistic development on cognition by referring to research done on reasoning with adults. His primary focus, however, is on the influence upon cognitive style of non-linguistic perceptual factors. He feels that the trend today appears to be a movement away from competence theory and toward performance theory. Performance theory is concerned with functions of language in everyday use and with non-linguistic as well as linguistic determinants. Thus Osgood, in essence, believes that any competence theory must be complemented by a theory that accounts for performance-type criteria. Osgood goes on to warn us against being overcritical of the behaviorists:

> "Many linguists and psycholinguists use behaviorism as a whipping boy these days — which is not really abnormal in scientific controversy, of course! But unfortunately (and polemically) they usually select the most simple and unsophisticated model of the opposing paradigm — the one most often presented to sophomores in Introductory Psychology. Only rarely are the more complex versions of behaviorism (even those of Hull and Tolman in the 1930's and '40's) or of more recent neobehaviorism — like those of Mowrer (cf. his 1960 Learning Theory and the Symbolic Processes) or even my own earlier elaboration (cf. my Method and Theory in Experimental Psychology 1953, and "Behavior Theory and the Social Sciences," 1956) — analysed in any detail."

In answering the first question, Piaget explains the importance of epistemology, interpretation, models, constructivism, structures, and symbolic functions. He emphasizes that the relationship between thought and language cannot be viewed clearly without a strong conception of the epistemology that supports its consequent interpretation. He elaborates upon the relationship between structures, symbolic function, and language. Additionally, he presents a critical overview of Chomsky's theory of language, comparing the Piagetian interpretation of the basis of language with the Chomskian view, as follows:

> "The fundamental difference between Chomsky and us is that we consider all cognitive acquisitions including language, to be the outcome of a gradual process of construction starting with the evolutionary forms of biological embryogenesis and ending up with modern scientific ideas. We thus reject the concept of preprogramming in any strict sense. What we consider as innate, however, is the general ability to synthesize the successive levels reached by the increasingly complex cognitive organization."

Neisser begins his interview by stating that cognition is a prerequisite for the acquisition and development of language. Cognition

lays the groundwork for verbal behavior. He continues by stating
that cognition and language development are completely interwoven.

Neisser proposes that in the early stages of development a
child perceives in terms of objects and events. Information about
his world is picked up by both vision and audition at first. There
is little separation between speech and gestures.

He admits that it is hard to pinpoint exactly where a child's
understanding begins. Understanding what is said about an object,
action, or person seems to be an integral part of comprehending that
object, action, or person itself. In more specific terms, the
spoken name of an object becomes an inseparable part of that object
for the child.

Kinsbourne believes that language acquisition depends on
cognitive development. Using the process of nominalization to
illustrate this, he points out that words are initially used in the
context of experiencing events. Specifically, there is a mapping
of words on external reality. As a child matures, a degree of
independence of the linguistic system from events evolves, and only
at this time does it become possible to mentally manipulate verbal
forms (i.e., map words onto words). Maturation of the brain is
emphasized as providing the potential and the opportunity for
behavioral advancement, that is, movement to more complex behavioral
levels.

In answering the question whether linguistic factors influence
cognitive development, Kinsbourne points out that words (vocabulary
and phraseology) limit, yet focus one's pattern of thought.

Discussion:

In reflecting upon the answers to this question, it would be
of great value to understand that although we use the terms language
and cognition as if they were separate entities in the mental
operations of the organism, they are best understood as the functions
of an interacting mental gestalt. Assuming that the above position
is valid it is still to be empirically determined what this dynamic
relationship of language and thought consists of and how it functions.
Even though this question is still an unanswered one, it appears
clear from our perspective that the most useful theoretical frame
of reference would be one which attempts to understand the reciprocal
relationship between language and thought as a functional,
dialectical relationship. From primarily a diachronic perspective,
it would seem to be important that we appreciate the role that
development plays in shaping the psychological relationship between
language and cognition as well as the epistemological issues
inherent in these two concepts. It is certainly clear that a great
deal more understanding and clarification is needed in order for

us to understand the dynamic relationship inherent in the mental
operation of language and thought.

QUESTION 2

In dealing with the question of the influence of verbal and
nonverbal behavior on the acquisition and development of language,
Chomsky feels that before a child can refer to an object there must
be the capacity to isolate and identify the object within the
context of its environment. Without this capacity and consequent
organization, the individual essentially has nothing to refer to.
Chomsky strongly supports the genetic determination of these
capacities — in other words, he does not think that there is any
reason to believe that these capacities are learned. He emphasizes
that to understand the growth of language, which is in itself highly
specific, one must consider the structural and functional properties
of this linguistic system as it grows and matures. In discussing
the relationship between structure and function in the development
of the linguistic system, he draws a striking parallel with the
relationship between structure and function in a bird learning to
fly: "We have something analogous to the incipient motions of the
fluttering of the wings of a bird before its capacity to fly has
matured."

Chomsky goes on to discuss two elementary properties of
language in terms of their relative importance: 1. the existence
of a discrete infinity, and 2. the rules of language that operate
on phrases.

In considering how language acquisition and development is
influenced by interpersonal and intrapersonal behavior Osgood
reaffirms his belief in the importance of pre-linguistic perceptual
cognizing. Most basic in pre-linguistic cognizing is the acquisition
of three basic semantic distinctions: Substantivity (distinguishing
palpable entities from impalpable relations); Directionality
(distinguishing cognitively prior SNPs from subsequent ONPs and
naturally ordered relations (e.g., actives) from unnaturally ordered
relations (e.g., passives)); and Stativity (distinguishing states
(FIGURE/STATE/GROUND) from actions (SOURCE/ACTION/RECIPIENT)).

In dealing with question two, Piaget uses the medium of symbolic
function and signs to stress the importance of interindividual
factors for mastery and development of language. Symbols, he
contends, lie somewhere between interpersonal and intrapersonal
behavior:

"In effect, we find symbols which have a conventional or
social meaning and symbols which have a meaning only for the
individual. In fact, since symbols are motivated by the
object, they may be created by the child himself and for his

use only. This clearly points to intrapersonal verbal and
nonverbal behavior. The first symbols of the child's play
are individual creations and yet all symbols bear a nonarbitrary relationship with the objects they designate. This
distinction is important; symbols can be socially shared or
they can be the result of the child's own creativity. Thus
the symbol presents an intermediary situation."

Neisser deals with the question of preverbal cognition by
comparing human research and animal studies. Focusing on simple
examples of behavior (i.e., solving detour problems, reaching for
a specific object), it has been shown that animals can understand
and perform tasks without the use of language. He believes that this
can be applied to the understanding of pre-verbal cognition in humans.

One of the main points made in this section was that infants
do not learn the names of things, but discover the structure of
language as well. Discovery, Neisser proposes, necessitates a
prepared mind. This opens the door for research in evaluating how
much and what kinds of preparation are needed for language development.

Another proposal was that comprehension of an object, action,
or person precedes the production of language. The example of
learning a second language illustrates this point, as it is recognized that most persons understand more than they actually verbalize.
A continuation of this thought is the statement that it is not
necessary to perform meaningful actions in order to perceive and
understand these actions. To crystallize this idea, Neisser provides
the following analogy between dancing and speaking:

"A dancer moves; a person watching the dance picks up information about the movements from what Gibson (1966) calls the
optic array. That is, the optical patterns available to the
viewer's eye specify the movements that a dancer has made.
‘Similarly a speaker executes movements in his mouth and
throat; a listener then picks up information about these
movements from what we might call the accoustic array. The
sound patterns available to the listener's ear specify the
articulatory movements of the speaker."

Finally, a rather novel approach is presented as an extension
of the above-mentioned method for the perception of actions. In
order to perceive and truly understand any action, Neisser believes
that it is necessary to be able to anticipate or to imagine what
will appear next in the sequence of an action. He refers to this
structured anticipation of information as an explanation for what
most people refer to as mental imagery.

Kinsbourne states that he does not view play as a form of
practice to master behavior, nor is he convinced that it is essential
for a child to fully realize his potential at a particular level of
behavioral development in order to progress to the next level.
Kinsbourne states:

"It becomes clear that theories which attribute developmental
disabilities to failure to act out a particular level of
motor development cannot be correct and remedial methods
based on them are therefore irrational. It is the sequence of
brain maturation, generating evermore sophisticated behavioral
potential that matters, not whether at any particular point
the potential was fully realized in action or not."

Discussion:

One of the most important issues raised by this question deals
with the nature of the symbolic or semiotic functions inherent in
the complex relationship between language and communication. Although
disagreement may exist among authorities as to the nature of symbolic
function during development, it is our opinion that symbolic function
serves as a mediating device between actions (i.e. preverbal intelligence) and representations (i.e. verbal intelligence). There is even
greater controversy among authorities as to the origin or moment of
acquisition of language and thought in the course of its on-going
development. Basic to the understanding of all this is the issue of
continuity versus discontinuity. From an historical perspective
there have been many controversies centered around this issue. Nevertheless, at the present time there is considerable disagreement
regarding the role that continuity and discontinuity play in human
development. In order to clarify where and when continuity versus
discontinuity may be useful in one's description of the development
of the human organism, it is most important to specify and be aware
of the epistemological differences that emerge when one describes a
particular event. Furthermore, it is crucial that we appreciate the
differences that make a difference when we are describing similar
things at various levels of abstraction.

If one considers the qualitative changes that occur in children
in terms of the process of their mental construction of the "real
world," the concept of discontinuity seems to be most useful. For
example, between the ages of four to six, the child readily engages
in what psychologists sometimes refer to as magical thinking, that
is an understanding of cause and effect relationships in a non-
logical manner. On the other hand, at about seven years of age
children begin to establish as a part of their understanding of the
real world a more logical relationship between cause and effect.

Another basic issue which is very much related to this concerns
the relationship between inner language as opposed to interpersonal

communicative discourse. Without a solid basis for inner language
events, children would not easily develop interpersonal communications, communication which is absolutely necessary for adequate
socialization. In this sense we may better understand inner language
as a by-product of the child's personal representations of his own
world. Furthermore, we may also more clearly understand his interpersonal world where cultural determinants play a significant role.

QUESTION 3

Two main points are emphasized in the discussion of the relationship of verbal and nonverbal systems. Although Chomsky claims to
have no real doctrine with regard to the interrelation of verbal and
nonverbal language systems, nevertheless, he speaks of the obvious
interconnections between these systems. Gestural systems are
specifically noted and thoroughly discussed as being associated with
spoken language.

The main thrust of this question centers around a discussion of
the meaning of the term "psychological reality." Chomsky clearly
takes a rationalist's position in discussing this topic — that is
to say psychological reality is not a matter of one truth versus
another truth, nor is it a matter of the quality of evidence or the
relevance of a particular theory. A theoretical approach or an
hypothesis facilitates one's ability to explain the facts or the way
things "really are." Chomsky maintains that there is a clear
distinction between psychological evidence (i.e. reaction time) and
psychological reality which does not have to be manifested by
empirical data. According to Chomsky the problem of psychological
reality boils down to a matter of rationality versus irrationality.
When it is truely rational, then it is psychologically real. To
clarify the term "psychological reality," Chomsky describes a study
performed by Sapir who:

"was looking at phonetic data from a certain American Indian
language and was able to show that if he assumed a certain
abstract phonological structure with rules of various kinds,
he could account for properties of these data. He could
explain some of the facts of language. That investigation
in itself was an investigation of psychological reality in
the only meaningful sense of the term....That is, he was
making a claim about psychological reality, and he had
evidence for it. The evidence was that his hypothesis
would explain some facts. And that is the only sense in
which there ever is evidence to support a truth-claim about
reality - physical or psychological. In fact, the so-called
'psychological evidence,' the behavioral evidence that
Sapir adduced was arguably weaker than the so-called
'linguistic evidence' adduced with regard to the correctness
of the abstract theory."

The relationships between verbal and nonverbal systems are illustrated in several ways in Osgood's response to the third question. The importance of the cognizing of entities prior to the cognizing of words is reaffirmed. Additionally, he refers to two neobehavioristic principles, the "Emic" and "Ambiguity" principles. Applying these principles to linguistics, three conclusions are derived: (1) cognitive systems are semantic in nature; (2) these systems are shared by both perceptual and linguistic information processing channels; and (3) natural "sentencing" is always context-dependent.

Piaget believes that verbal and nonverbal systems are inter-related. To demonstrate this point, he considers the relative importance of representational thought, sensorimotor coordination, imitation (deferred imitation), symbolic function, and knowledge.

For Neisser, one of the most important interrelationships between verbal and nonverbal signal systems is acquired when language gives meaning and understanding to actions.

In answering question three, Kinsbourne proposes a relationship between the acquisition and development of language and the maturation of the brain. As the brain matures, an individual becomes able to move along a particular response hierarchy, and as a result, becomes increasingly able to overcome innately formed "preprogrammed" response tendencies, and use other response patterns, even if they conflict with those that conform least to the brain's inherent information. Kinsbourne provides us with the example of a concert pianist who has learned to overcome "preprogrammed" finger sequences (e.g. 1-2-3-6 or vice versa) by learning new patterns of finger movement. The pianist has moved along a response hierarchy, and with practice, has minimized innate restraints.

Discussion:

There is little doubt among most authorities that there is an intrinsic relationship between the verbal and nonverbal signals. To the extent that nonverbal language is the dominant mode of communication at earlier pre-linguistic stages of development, this condition provides a hierarchial constraint in the organism with the consequence that one cannot have language without thought. Never-theless, it is quite clear that from a developmental perspective thought is always possible without language. This has been demon-strated time and time again with studies on the verbal and cognitive abilities of deaf children.

QUESTION   4

Responding to the nature/nurture question, Chomsky points out that our genetic-biological endowment contributes significantly to the growth and structure of language. This is not to say however, that environment has no influence at all. Chomsky believes that the problem is to tease out the distinct contributions of both biology and environment. He also distinguishes between the influence of a triggering effect and shaping effect on the linguistic system, and states that these also must be understood as to their unique contributions. He freely admits that he may have tended to slight and underestimate the environmental factors.

Concerning his description of the linguistic system as a mental organ, Chomsky proposes the following assumptions: 1. the system of language is very complex - its complexity goes beyond the assumption of the physical origin of language, and 2. the language system is essentially uniform over a significant range of individuals. With this in mind, he believes that the basic properties of the linguistic system are genetically determined. This is the only feasible way, according to Chomsky, to account for the specific structure and uniform growth of the linguistic system in man.

To crystallize his views on the relative influence of "nature versus nurture" on language and cognition generally, Osgood offers a condensed version of his proposed criteria for anything being a language (6) and for something being a human language (an additional 10 criteria). Criteria one through six refer to (1) non-random recurrency of forms, (2) reciprocality in producing and receiving, (3) pragmatics (non-random form-behavior dependencies), (4) semantics (non-random rules of reference), (5) syntax (non-random rules of combining forms), and (6) combinatorial productivity (capability of producing infinite numbers of novel combinations which satisfy the above). The remaining 10 criteria supply additional structural and functional characteristics that serve to define something being a humanoid language (e.g. structural like use of the vocal-auditory channel; functional, like the arbitrariness of form/meaning relations).

In answering question four, Piaget emphasizes that the study of individuals suffering from pathological conditions of language and thought is essential — specifically when studying results which indicate that language does not constitute the framework of logic, but, rather is molded by logic.

Neisser prefaces his answer to the nature/nurture question by stating that the influence of genetic factors has turned out to be more powerful than originally expected. However, neither nature nor nurture plays the major role in language development; instead, there is an interaction between the two. He provides us with

several examples. Research on deaf children born to hearing parents,
who developed a language of structured referential sequences with
no 'environmental encouragement', lends credence to the influence
of innate genetic endowments for language development. Conversely,
attempts to teach various types of language to chimpanzees (Gardners,
Premack) have been less successful than they first appeared to be.
Research mentioned somewhat later in the conversation deals with the
work of Gallup with chimpanzees. Gallup experimented with the self-
recognition of chimpanzees in isolated and normal environments, and
then compared these results to similar work with monkeys. Conclusions from this work support Neisser's argument of the importance of
both environmental and genetic influence for linguistic development.
On the nature side of the argument, it was found that chimpanzees and
monkeys differ in their responses in similar testing situations.
To support the nurture side, differences were noted between responses
of the chimpanzees raised in an isolated environment as compared to
a normal environment. The above experiments reaffirm Neisser's
belief that it is vital to understand the interaction between the
environmental and genetic aspects of language development and
cognition.

At this point in the discussion, Neisser diverges somewhat by
pointing out that language has other functions aside from describing
external events. He believes that feelings are important in giving
rise to both language and cognition, saying:

"It is clear...that emotion and communication are related.
All the social animals communicate, and some of the main
things they signal to one another are what they intend to
do next: fight, flee, submit, engage in sexual behavior.
It is not unreasonable to call these intentions their
'emotions'. They are signalled by gestures and movements
of every kind. It would be remarkable if the same thing
were not true of human beings."

In more specific terms, emotional signals are a form of communication for which we are biologically equipped. Neisser maintains
that individuals must be equipped with the right kind of nervous
system to be able to perceive what others are signifying in their
intentions. He points out the possibility that perhaps the problem
with autistic children is that they are not born with the appropriate
neural equipment, and as a result, are unable to understand others'
intentions.

The first part of question four, of what importance is the
biological basis of language perception and production, focuses on
individual differences in preprogramming of the brain for speech.
Kinsbourne postulates that as the control system in the brain
becomes increasingly differentiated, neurons in turn, lose connections. The consequence is that specific functions become more

localized with neuronal organization allowing for greater degrees
of differentiation. As a particular function becomes more differentiated, it also becomes further removed in "functional distance"
from the rest of the brain. Kinsbourne continues with this train
of thought by considering how a particular neuronal system which
controls some specific aspect of behavior would develop, and where
in the brain it would be located. Using a dual-task paradigm (a
test where two tasks are performed concurrently) to determine the
localization of function, he concludes that functions which
potentially interfere with each other, but have to be combined for
a final result, would be more effectively programmed if in different
portions of the brain, removed from each other in functional cerebral
distance. Conversely, those functions which work based on a common
programming principle, such as a common rhythm, should be more
closely connected, being separated by a smaller functional distance.
Speech and hearing are viewed as the latter type of functions.

Kinsbourne believes that pathological conditions have great
utility in the study of language and thought as they may help us to
better understand the components of normal language systems. He
mentions four examples: autism, aphasia, psychotic language, and
language of the deaf. Autism is interpreted as the inability to
map one's phonological system onto the cognitive system, resulting
in a situation where words lack reference. Research on autism will
give an understanding of how the linguistic system may develop
independently of any cognitive basis. Considering aphasia,
Kinsbourne believes that a clearer understanding of the site and
nature of brain lesions in aphasics that interfere with verbal
expression and comprehension, will be helpful in explaining the
neurological basis of language. He points out that:

> "When a person is aphasic, has he lost the ability to
> communicate verbally or has he lost the ability to communi-
> cate in any form whatever? Is it a problem of verbal
> signalling or a more broadly defined problem of symbolic
> behavior? This can be tested by determining what a person
> with global aphasia can still learn to do in order to
> communicate...We find that meta-languages such as writing
> and morse code are indeed lost, but that sign and gestural
> language as forms of expression are maintained. This
> teaches us that communicative systems are not all represented
> in the same place, but rather that verbal communication and
> gestural communication are differently represented."

Research with psychotic language will give a clearer view of how
language maps onto cognition (the cognitive defect being primary in
this case). Finally, the study of the deaf will aid in the understanding of the importance of verbal expression for intellectual
cognitive development.

Discussion:

Almost any question regarding human nature poses the inevitable debate of the relative weight of the predisposing genetically-endowed factors versus the learned culturally-determined factors. In terms of pounds per paragraph, the polemics centering on this issue outweigh any other. Nevertheless, any conclusive answer regarding the importance of one or the other has not been forth coming. It is more than likely that in spite of the fact that even though we do not have adequate ability to separate or control the variables necessary to answer this question, much of the confusion in this debate has resulted from a failure to sufficiently understand and/or acknowledge the dynamic interactions between biological, sociological, and psychological dimensions of the life of the mind. This psychologically leads us to the age old question as to what constitutes normal behavior. For an adequate answer to this question it would be best to postulate normal behavior as being on a continuum with abnormal behavior, in other words, normal and abnormal behavior are on the extremes of a single dimension. Given this epistemological framework, it becomes apparent that the better one can understand the extremes of the continuum, the better one will be able to understand the shades of gray in between. Here the study of how deaf children think and speak throws light on similar processes in normal children. Similarly, the study of brain-damaged children suffering from developmental aphasia and the study of adults suffering from acquired aphasia will help us in our understanding of delayed and disordered language acquisition in normal and non-brain injured children. Here the possibility clearly exists to further explore and understand the possible existence of parallels between levels of language, learning, and degrees or stages of language disturbances.

QUESTION 5

Chomsky supports the work with chimpanzees and apes as a method to understand the intellectual capacity of these species, although he mentions that this method may not be the most effective with which to obtain results. His most assertive belief concerning this topic is that the rudimentary capabilities of human language are beyond the capacities of apes. Further on in the dialogue, Chomsky deals with this question in terms of what he calls a biological paradox. He poses the following question — namely, "Suppose an organism has a certain capability with circumstances selectively advantageous and favorable, but never used this capability?" Chomsky uses the answer to this question to reinforce and substantiate his claims on this topic.

Osgood applaudes the work with chimpanzees in the field of psycholinguistics, stating that research in this area has been long overdue. Using his definitions for anything being a language — as previously described in the interview — he evaluates the work done

with chimpanzees and sign language, particularly the Gardner's work
with Washoe. He concludes that five of his six fundamental criteria
(questions (1) through (4) plus (6)) for the determination of something qualifying as a language are clearly fulfilled. However, he
points out that criterion (5), dealing with syntax, may be the stum-
ling block for the classifying of Washoe's signings as being a
language. Nevertheless, the comparison with two areas of human
linguistic development — the development of complexity of "utterances" and the responses to WH-questions (who, what, when and where) —
Osgood thinks provides "proof" that, indeed, Washoe's communications
may be classified as a language. He strongly suggests that this lends
credence to questioning the distance usually assumed between the
cognitive capacities of humans and other higher primates. It is self-
deceptive and arrogant for humans to consider themselves purely
rational beings superior to animals he cautions:

> "Let me emphasize again: these „gut„ dynamics of human
> thinking and talking — Affective Polarity effects,
> Congruence Dynamics (psychologic), and Pollyandism —
> are not „rational„ processes, and they operate (usually
> beyond awareness) on people in high places as well as low.
> The sooner human beings stop kidding themselves that they
> are, unlike other animals, purely rational beings à la
> Descartes and accept the fact that they carry along a
> Neanderthal within — the sooner they'll be able to think
> and act more rationally (as paradoxical as that may seem!)
> and improve their prospects in this nuclear age for reaching
> and going beyond the year 2000."

In the fifth question in which work with chimpanzees and apes
using sign language is considered, Piaget mentions the existence
of a possible continuity within the evolutionary spectrum.

> "It is clear that there exists the possibility of a real
> continuity within the evolutionary system. In genetic
> epistemology, in developmental psychology or within the
> biological range, we can never reach a point where we can
> say that 'here is the beginning of logical structure'.
> As soon as we start talking about the general coordination
> of actions, we find ourselves going even further back into
> the area of biology."

Neisser interprets studies with apes and chimpanzees as
advantageous for gaining a better persepction of ourselves, specifically in terms of more clearly understanding what "equipment" we,
as humans, have been given, and what role in cognition these
endowments play.

Kinsbourne believes that the research in comparative psycholinguistics which attempts to understand how the intellectual

abilities of apes and chimpanzees contracts with the mental abilities
of humans is valuable, and should continue. However, he believes
that the ability to classify these species' communications as a
language is not a crucial issue, and would depend upon the criteria
and consequently, the definitions one uses to classify behavior as
a language.

Discussion:

The eighteenth century French philosopher LaMettrie rejected
the long-cherished notion of man's uniqueness on the grounds that
man was a machine and seemed to him to differ merely in degree, not
in kind from other animals. LaMettrie's belief in the continuity
of animal and human intelligence led him to speculate especially on
experiments similar to current research in teaching an ape to speak.
The continuity/discontinuity problem does not seem to be an issue
when dealing solely with animals on the phylogenetic scale below
homo sapiens. However, the issue of continuity between man and other
animals on the scale has been a perennial problem from Aristotle
right up to the present. Much of the problem here centers upon an
epistemological issue of the definition of language. Until such
time as sufficient scientific information will be available and
acceptable to the leading authorities in this field that will enable
us to conclusively define the meaning of language, little agreement
among such authorities will be forthcoming.

QUESTION 6

The focus of the last two questions moves away from direct
issues within the field of language and cognition to broader considerations such as applications and future developments.

Chomsky does not venture a detailed answer to the question of
the most important and promising applications of research in the
field of the psychology of language and cognition, as he feels he
has limited experience in this area. Instead, he suggests that
practitioners (e.g. therapists and teachers) should be the persons
to develop this line of thought and research.

In answering the sixth question, Osgood expressed his concern
that both linguistics and cognitive psychology are plagued by the
problem of "faddism". This he believes, is evidenced in both the
topics "of the day" and the "approved" methods of research, and even
as well in underlying theoretical assumptions (often unexpressed and
even out of awareness!). The really serious effect of such
"faddism", of course, is that perfectly good research in "non-fad"
areas has trouble seeing the light of published day!

Piaget stresses the importance and relevancy of any new theory
of cognitive development being interdisciplinary in nature. He

states that the most promising aspect seems to be in the development
of suitable explanations. Considering linguistics, Piaget believes
that the relationship between linguistics and logic is important,
and in the remaining part of the question, deals with the means with
which this theory may be developed.

Neisser mentions four sources of new perspectives for research
in the field of language and cognition: cross-cultural research,
studies of infancy, work with animals, and studies in artificial
intelligence. He views cross-cultural research as having a critical
role in the understanding of cognitive development. It appears that
research in language development and cognition is influenced by two
factors: maturation and formal schooling. Cross-cultural studies
would be able to clarify the influence of both aspects mentioned
above by controlling for the effects of schooling and cultural bias.

Kinsbourne feels that the field of psychology of language and
cognition is still within a "Linnean" phase, a stage where measurement and classification are given maximum emphasis. He states:

"It seems to me that psychology is at this time in what
might be called a pre-Darwinian phase, in a Linnean phase.
It is faculty psychology updated. Psychologists basically
did what Wundt did. They measure the limits of performance
in increasingly sophisticated ways....The problem is that
anybody can choose to measure whatever they please and without any particular reason Newell characterized this by
saying 'you can't play Twenty Questions with nature and win'."

Although advanced methodology is prevalent, he believes that this
field has a limited paradigm, and is essentially theoretical.
Research in mental functioning should focus on its two fundamental
ingredients: selection and construction. Kinsbourne proposes that
the study of these two aspects, especially at the neural level, will
provide answers in this field.

Discussion:

The application of scientific knowledge in the area of the
psychology of language and thought is useful to the extent that it
provides an adequate and meaningful intellectual frame of reference
for the explanation of the study of the mental life of the
individual. Furthermore, it is beneficial to the practitioner as a
belief system which may serve to provide a sense of purpose,
security, and faith in the methods used to bring about a change in
the individual. At the present time, the most prominent applications
of psycholinguistic research seem to be in the areas of second
language learning, better instruction for children with reading
and related learning disabilities, and the rehabilitation of children
and adults with speech, language, and thinking disorders.

QUESTION 7

    Chomsky mentions several related points in the final question. He believes that his major contribution to the field has been in the application of the "cannons of rationality" which has been taken for granted in the natural sciences. He believes that Skinner's approach represents a methodology opposite to his own.

> "Skinner departs radically from the framework of the
> natural sciences in several important ways; specifically,
> by taking it as an a priori principle that you're not
> allowed to develop abstract theories. As he puts it,
> you're not allowed to develop theories of internal repres-
> entation or mental structure...."

Vehemently denouncing this approach, Chomsky contends that, "anyone who insists on this doctrine — merely a form of mysticism — is never going to get anywhere."

    In looking toward a new theory, he emphasizes the importance and validity of the study of the human mind and its growth using methods similar to those implemented in the natural sciences. He stresses the isolation of the sub-systems as well as the principles that govern structure, function, and their interactions. Finally, referring to himself as in the minority, Chomsky believes that it has been possible in the past several years to form a theory of language that has a deductive structure concomitant with a strong sense of unification and explanatory power.

    In responding to the final question, Osgood expressed his belief that, indeed, psycholinguistics is in a state of transition, in search of a new paradigm. Of course, he thinks his research and theorizing on an Abstract Performance Grammar (APG) is a valid direction for the interdisciplinary field to explore. He feels that the people in psycholinguistics are generating models that are closer to actual language performance in real life communication situations. He does not preclude the fact that older communication models must be taken into account (i.e. Chomsky's Abstract Competence Grammar), but rather he emphasizes that the new direction is consistent with his own research and theorizing. With this in mind, Osgood gives a brief overview of his (recently-published, 1980) book, Lectures on Language Performance — an anticipation of his planned volume, to be titled Toward an Abstract Performance Grammar — many aspects of which have been emphasized in this interview.

    For the final question, Piaget points out that any theory that emerges will be interdisciplinary in nature. He believes that the maintenance of an equilibrium as well as state of transition are essential for the survival and blossoming of any theory.

When asked if the field of language and cognition was searching for a new paradigm, Neisser emphasizes that this area has been and still is in a state of transition. Models of formal grammar and syntax have been studied. Work is now focusing on case grammars and pragmatics. He believes that work with mother/infant/family interactions will yield important conclusions for cognition and linguistic development.

"It is entirely reasonable to study language in the context where it naturally occurs. That is almost invariably in a social context, and for young children that means in the family. Perhaps it's odd that anyone ever thought of studying language any other way. The same point can be made not only for language but for cognitive processes in general. For too long we have been studying cognition in rather artificial laboratory settings. One can learn that way, but there comes a time when it is better to move back and get a better idea of what happens in ordinary life."

Turning to neuropsychology, it is evident that great strides have been made. However, Neisser feels that the contribution of neuropsychology to cognition and linguistics at this time is limited. He argues that understanding the structure of the brain requires first that we gain a greater understanding of the nature of language and thought:

"The brain is no less complicated than the world. There is an immensely complex system of millions of neurons, of chemical transmitters and electrical activity. We need a conceptualization of it. It's not enough to divide the brain into areas, with this area more important for x and that for y; we need to know how it works. There is not much chance of that in neuropsychology until we have a conception of language and thought that will suggest what kind of structure one should look for. Without that there will be as many alternative models of the complexities of the brain as we have of the complexities of the world around us."

Pointing towards the future, Neisser maintains that we will have to look at the sustained interaction between genetic and environmental influences to more clearly comprehend language development and cognition. In closing, he predicts that the future will hold new ideas — new in the sense of having different ways of considering previously suggested thoughts, and of having the capability to use these ideas in unanticipated depths.

Answering the final question, Kinsbourne maintains that the field of language and cognition is searching for a new theoretical basis. New theories should focus more on specific brain states that underlie cognition and its development. Only in this way will

it be possible for applications to go beyond species-specific
generalities to understanding how individuals differ.

Discussion:

It is clear at the present time that the status of the area of
the psychology of language and thought, often referred to as psycholinguistics, reflects the status of the field of psychology in
general. This condition is best understood as being in a state of
transition. The paradigms or theoretical frameworks (i.e.
behaviorism, Chomskian linguistics) which have had the most powerful
impact during the last forty years have lost their "real power,"
and are going through radical changes at the present time. Both
of these above-mentioned schools of thought and other groups
associated with these movements are attempting to reformulate and
reconstruct their positions so that they may exert a more viable
force during this period of transition. At the present time, there
is no one prevailing school of thought in psychology or psycholinguistics. All of this has widely opened the field to the possibility of new leadership. Currently, the present contenders for
this leadership seem to be cognitive psychology, especially the
developmentalists in this group, and neuropsychology. Whatever the
future may bring, it is clear that this current transition period
is quite crucial. The foundations for what is to come are presently
being planted and carefully cultivated. Let us hope that then
dangers of reductionism and the fallacies of conceiving of language
and mind as simple bi-products of brain mechanisms and/or bio-
chemistry are avoided. Moreover, let us also hope that a purely
neo-idealistic approach that reduces language and mind to pure
subjectivity and dismisses the body's neurophysiology and chemistry
as irrelevant is also avoided. The basic challenge here for the
future is to achieve a comprehensive unified approach that conceives
of language and mind within the organism or body in reciprocal
relationships and as a part of a common humanity of the social value
system of the culture.

Conclusion:

It has been our intention in this chapter to provide a brief
but cogent overview of the dialogues that follow in this book. We
hope that this succinct introduction will provide the basis for you,
the reader, better to appreciate the diverging points of view
provided by the five distinguished authorities interviewed.

PART II
DIALOGUES

DIALOGUE I

Noam Chomsky's Views on the
Psychology of Language and Thought

Noam Chomsky was born on December 7, 1928 in Philadelphia, Pennsylvania. His undergraduate and graduate years were spent at the University of Pennsylvania where he received his Ph.D. in linguistics in 1955. During the years 1951 to 1955 Chomsky was a Junior Fellow of the Harvard University Society of Fellows. While a Junior Fellow he completed his doctoral dissertation entitled, "Transformational Analysis." The major theoretical viewpoints of the dissertation appeared in the monograph Syntactic Structures, which was published in 1957. This formed part of a more extensive work, The Logical Structure of Linguistic Theory, circulated in mimeograph in 1955 and published in 1975.

Chomsky joined the staff of the Massachusetts Institute of Technology in 1955 and in 1961 was appointed full professor in the Department of Modern Languages and Linguistics (now the Department of Linguistics and Philosophy) and in the Research Laboratory of Electronics. In 1966 he was appointed to the Ferrari P. Ward Professorship of Modern Languages and Linguistics. In 1976 he was appointed Institute Professor.

During the years 1958 to 1959 Chomsky was in residence at the Institute for Advanced Study at Princeton, New Jersey. In 1962 he was appointed a Research Fellow in Cognitive Studies at the Center for Cognitive Studies of Harvard University. In the summer of 1966 he served as Linguistic Society of America Professor at the Linguistic Institute, University of California, Berkeley. In the spring of 1969 he delivered the John Locke Lectures at Oxford and the Shearman Lectures at University College, London; in January 1970 he delivered the Bertrand Russell Memorial Lectures at Cambridge University, London. In 1972 he delivered the Nehru Lecture in New Delhi, and in 1977, the Huizinga Lecture in Leiden.

Professor Chomsky has received honorary degrees at the University of London, University of Chicago, Loyola University of Chicago, Swarthmore College, Delhi University, Bard College, and the University of Massachusetts. He is a Fellow of the American Academy of Arts and Sciences and a member of the National Academy of Science. In addition, he is a member of other professional and learned societies in the United States and abroad.

Chomsky is the author of books and articles on linguistics, philosophy, intellectual history, and contemporary issues. These include: Aspects of the Theory of Syntax, Cartesian Linguistics, Sound Pattern of English (with M. Halle), Language and Mind, Studies on Semantics in Generative Grammar, At War With Asia, American Power and the New Mandarins, Problems of Knowledge and Freedom, For Reasons of State, Peace in the Middle East?, Reflections on Language, Essays on Form and Interpretation, 'Human Rights' and American Foreign Policy, Language and Responsibility, The Political Economy of Human Rights, 2 Volumes, (with E. S. Herman), Lectures on Government and Binding: The Pisa Lectures, and Towards a New Cold War (forthcoming).

Dialogue I. Noam Chomsky's Views on the Psychology of Language and Thought

I.   What role does cognition play in the acquisition and the development of language? Do linguistic factors influence general cognitive development?

CHOMSKY: I would like to re-phrase the first question and ask what role other aspects of cognition play in the acquisition and development of language since, as put, it is not a question I can answer, I would want to regard language as one aspect of cognition and its development as one aspect of the development of cognition. It seems to me that, what we can say in general is this:-

There are a number of cognitive systems which seem to have quite distinct and specific properties. These systems provide the basic for certain cognitive capacities — for simplicity of expo- sition, I will ignore the distinction and speak — a bit misleadingly about cognitive capacities. The language faculty is one of these cognitive systems. There are others. For example, our capacity to organize visual space, or to deal with abstract properties of the number system, or to comprehend and appreciate certain kinds of musical creation, or our ability to make sense of the social structures in which we play a role, which undoubtedly reflects conceptual structures that have developed in the mind, and any number of other mental capacities. As far as I can see, to the extent that we understand anything about these capacities they appear to have quite specific and unique properties. That is, I don't see any obvious relationship between, for example, the basic properties of the structure of language as represented in the mind on the one hand, and the properties of our capacity, say, to recognise faces or understand some situation in which we play a role, or appreciate music and so on. These seem to be quite different

33

and unique in their characteristics. Furthermore, every one of
these mental capacities appears to be highly articulated as well as
specifically structured. Now, it's perfectly reasonable to ask how
the development of one of these various systems relates to the
development of others. Similarly, in the study of, say, the physical
growth of the body, it makes perfect sense to ask how the development
of one system relates to the development of others. Let's say, how
the development of the circulatory system relates to the development
of the visual system.

But, in the study of the physical body, nobody would raise a
question analogous to the one you posed in quite this form. That
is, we would not ask what role physical organs and their function
play in the development of the visual system. Undoubtedly, there
are relations between say the visual and circulatory systems, but
the way we approach the problem of growth and development in the
physical body is rather different. That is, one asks — quite
properly — what are the specific properties and characteristics of
the various systems that emerge, how do these various organs or
systems interact with one another, what is the biological basis —
the genetic coding, ultimately — that determines the specific
pattern of growth, function and interaction of these highly articulated systems: for instance, the circulatory system, the visual
system, the liver, and so on. And that seems to provide a reasonable analogy, as a point of departure at least, for the study of
cognitive development and cognitive structure, including the growth
of the language faculty as a special case.

RIEBER: It might help if you could define how you use the term
"cognition" as opposed to the term "language."

CHOMSKY: Well, I wouldn't use the term "cognition" as _opposed_
to the term "language." Rather, cognition is an overall term that
includes every system of belief, knowledge, understanding, interpretation, perception, and so on. Language is just one of many
systems that interact to form our whole complex of cognitive
structures. So it's not a matter of language as _compared_ with
cognition any more than one could study, say, our knowledge of the
structure of visual space as compared with cognition. Furthermore,
I don't believe that one can think of "cognition" as a unitary
phenomenon.

RIEBER: Cognition is a way of knowing and language is a medium
whereby we know?

CHOMSKY: Not as I am using the terms, the term "cognition" as
far as I understand it simply refers to any aspect of our belief,
knowledge, or understanding. Now among the various cognitive systems
and cognitive structures, one of them happens to be the system of
language. We know language more or less as we have a system of
beliefs and understanding about, say, the nature of the visual world.

RIEBER: So it's a separate system is it not?

CHOMSKY: It's one of the many systems entering into an array
of interconnected cognitive structures. Perhaps the analogy to
physical organs is the best way to explain the way I see it. Let's
just ask how do we study the structure of the body. We begin by a
process of idealization, in effect. We say there are — we assume
there are — various systems that interact to constitute our physical
body. For example, the visual system and the circulatory system and
so on. Now this is, of course, an idealization; the systems are not
physically separable. The circulatory system interacts with the
visual system physically.

RIEBER: But the CNS and the ANS are separable....

CHOMSKY: Only under a certain idealization, which is assumed
to be an appropriate one. Well, you can study the structure of each
of these systems and the mode of their interaction. Everyone assumes
that this is a proper way to study anything as complicated as the
human body: by isolating for investigation particular systems that
have their own specific structure and a specific mode of development,
recognizing of course that they are not isolated from one another —
that the mode of their interaction is just as much genetically determined as are their specific characteristics. So, using the term
"organ" in a slightly extended sense to include something like, say,
the circulatory system — not the usual sense — we might regard the
body as a system of physical organs, each with its specific properties and peculiarities and with a mode of interaction, all genetically determined in basic outline, but modified in various ways in
the course of growth. Now, I think that there is every reason to
suppose that the same kind of "modular" approach is appropriate for
the study of the mind — which I understand to be the study at an
appropriate level of abstraction of properties of the brain — and
in particular for the general system of cognitive structures, which
does not exhaust the mind, but is the part we're talking about.
That is to say, I'd like to think of the system of cognitive
structures as in effect a system of "mental organs," each of which
is quite specific, highly articulated, developing in a particular
manner that is intrinsically determined — if the biologists are
right, genetically coded — with, of course, complex interactions
that are also very largely predetermined. It seems to me that,
insofar as we understand anything about cognition — about some
aspects of cognition — we discover very specific mental structures
developing in the course of growth and maturation in quite their own
way. And language is simply one of these structures. I'm sure if
we were to study, to take another distinctly human characteristic,
our capacity to deal with properties of the number system — it's
unique to humans, as far as we know, a specific capacity of the
human mind — one might, for example, try to explore the properties
of that system in the mature person. We might then ask how that

system develops through childhood, what kind of stimulation from
the environment is necessary for it to develop to its mature state,
and so on. In doing so we would have studied the growth of a
particular mental organ to its mature state, and if we could pursue
this enterprise successfully, we could, at least on an abstract
level, characterize the principles that determine the structure of
this mental organ, principles that must be themselves genetically
coded in some fashion. (The language system can be and, in fact,
is being studied in essentially this way. Similarly, we could study
the other mental organs that I mentioned before or others.) In this
way we could develop what seems to me a reasonable version of a
"faculty psychology."

RIEBER: When you talk about this language structure system,
are you referring to all language nonverbal language and language
as a developmental process?

CHOMSKY: Here we have to be a little careful. The term
"language" is used in quite different ways, and only confusion can
arise from failure to distinguish them. In the first place, the
term is used to refer to human languages, that is, a specific
biological characteristic of humans. There is a human language
faculty which allows us to develop the kind of knowledge that you
and I share that makes it possible for us to conduct this conversation. And that capacity is simply part of the species-specific
biological endowment. Putting aside possible individual variation,
we may think of this faculty as common and as far as we know uniquely
human possession. In terminology that is now fairly standard, we
may refer to a characterization of central properties of this faculty
as "universal grammar," a system that we may regard as analogous to
basic properties of the human visual system. That is one use of the
term "language." Each human language is one of the various specific
systems that can emerge within that set of initial constraints. The
term "language" is often used in quite a different way, referring
not to some specific biologically determined system, but rather to
any mode of communication or mode of expression, in some very general
sense. So, for example, when one talks about the language of gesture
or the language of the bees, or the language of ape calls, or when
one asks whether music is a language or mathematics is a language
and so on, in any of those questions and discussions, some notion of
"language" is presupposed which is very different from the former
sense.

RIEBER: I was really thinking of something else. I was thinking of the notion that some people believe, namely that oral
language, verbal language in the child is a development of something
that happens prior to the emergence of spoken language — nonverbal
activities such as pointing, etc., cognitive activity — pre-
language rites as it were.

II. *How is the acquisition and development of language influenced*
     by interpersonal and intrapersonal verbal and nonverbal
     behavior?

CHOMSKY: It depends on what aspect of language one is talking
about.

RIEBER: Say, the first word, for instance.

CHOMSKY: Let's take the first word and assume that it's a name.
Suppose the child's first word is some name for its mother, or something like that. In the act of reference, obviously other cognitive
capacities come into play. That is, before a child can refer to some
object in its external environment, it has to have isolated and
identified objects in its environment. It has to have recognized
that there are people, that there are things, and that they have
certain properties — constancies and persistence and so on. Unless
all of this organization has already taken place, there is nothing
to refer to. Therefore, the act of reference can't take place. I
don't think there is any special reason to believe that any of those
competences are learned. I assume that the capacities that enable
us to isolate and identify physical objects in the outside world and
understand their properties — capacities which we might also think
of as forming some mental organ — are just as much genetically
determined in their specific characteristics as is the language
faculty. But there is no doubt that in, for example, using a word
to refer to an object, that kind of organization is presupposed,
however it is developed. That's almost tautological. So in that
respect, of course, other cognitive capacities enter crucially into
any use of language, including the earliest use. However, that
doesn't tell us very much. To take a physical analogy, we might also
say that unless the circulatory system is functioning, the visual
system is inoperative. It's perfectly correct, but it doesn't tell
us anything about the structure of the visual system. The kind of
question that ought to be raised in connection with the growth of
language is just the kind of question that we raise in connection
with the growth of some other system, say, the visual system. What
are the structural and functional properties that emerge as this
system grows and matures? What are the principles that govern this
growth and that are realized in the systems that develop? To what
extent are these principles invariant and biologically determined?
To what extent do the properties of the system that develops simply
mirror accidental contingencies of experience? To what extent do
they reflect other independently developing capacities, and so on.)
I think that as far as we know the growth and emergence of the
language faculty is highly specific. By the time the child has the
most rudimentary knowledge of language, say at three years old, a
normal child — and in fact any child, apart from really serious
pathology — is using principles that as far as we know have no close
analogue in other mental faculties. After all, what are the basic

properties of language, the most rudimentary and elementary
properties of language, which emerge quite early — certainly a four-
year-old has already developed them very extensively. The most
elementary property of language that one can think of, I guess, is
that it involves a discrete infinity; that is, there is an infinite
range of possible constructions — there is no longest sentence.
This is not a continuous system, that is, it does not involve variation along some continuous dimension, as say the bee language does
in principle; but rather there is a discrete infinity of possible
expressions, each with its form and its meaning. That property of
language manifests itself at an extremely early point. Prior to
this point one might want to say that there is no language in the
sense of "human language." Prior to that point it would make sense
to say that we have something analogous to the incipient motions of
fluttering of wings of a bird before its capacity to fly has matured,
perhaps. But at the point at which the system of a discrete infinity
of utterances manifests itself, and that's very early, we can say
that we have at least the rudiments of human language emerging. As
for the principles that organize and characterize that discrete
infinity of utterances with their forms and meaning, obviously this
system must be represented in a finite mind — ultimately, neurally
represented in a finite brain — which means that there must be
some finite system of rules which operate in some fashion to
characterize the unbounded range of possible expressions, each with
its fixed form and meaning. And knowledge of language means nothing
more than internal representation, ultimately neural representation
of that system. Perhaps the next most elementary property of
language is that these rules basically operate on phrases; that is,
they don't operate on a string of words, a sequence of words, but on
words organized into larger units. Then, as we go on to further
properties of language, we discover ways in which the rules operate
on phrases and on hierarchic structures of phrases in order to form
more complex expressions by recursive embedding and other principles.
As far as I can see, these are the most elementary properties of
human language. But even these elementary properties, so far as we
know — have no significant analogues in other systems.

There are, of course, quite different views of the matter.
Piaget and his colleagues, if I understand them, take the position
that the emerging structures of language necessarily reflect sensorimotor constructions. I have never understood exactly what they mean
by this claim. If they are saying, for example, that a child cannot
use words to refer without having something to refer to, that is,
without a prior organization of the world into objects of possible
reference, then one cannot object, obviously. But they seem to be
claiming something more, perhaps that the principles that govern the
structure and functioning of the language faculty are in fact
principles that arise in the course of the development of the child's
sensorimotor constructions. If that is the claim, then it seems to
me a very curious one, which cannot be maintained on the basis of

any current knowledge of the nature of these systems. Perhaps some
sense can be made of this claim, but I'm not aware of any formulation
of it that has any credibility at all, and I constantly wonder why
it is put forth with such dogmatic certainty. It seems to have
little prior plausibility, and to my knowledge lacks any empirical
support.

    RIEBER: Your metaphor of birds just reminded my that Leonardo
da Vinci wanted to study the structure of the bird in order to discover the functional dynamics of flying. In the study of the
structure of the bird was the key to what flight was, and it seems
that this approach is pretty much the same in general principle as
Leonardo's approach, i.e. from the study of structure comes the
knowledge of function.

    CHOMSKY: That's extremely natural. I can't imagine any other
approach. How else could one proceed?

    RIEBER: Well, some people feel that to study the other way
around perhaps is better. To study function in order to find out
what structure is. And, of course, that's what you were attacking
when you set out to destroy the house that Skinner built.

    CHOMSKY: Well, not really. My criticism of Skinner was not
that he was trying to study structure on the basis of function, but
rather that in the Skinnerian system there are simply no principles.
His "theory of language" was almost vacuous. I don't mean to say
that his principles of partial reinforcement, for example, are
vacuous; they are not. How interesting they are, one might argue,
but at least they have content. However, in the work that he's
done on so-called higher mental processes, for example language,
there are simply no discernible principles at all. When you explore
the proposals that he puts forth, they dissolve into metaphor and
vacuity. One can see very easily why this should be the case: it's
because Skinner departs radically from the framework of the natural
sciences in several important ways; specifically, by taking it as
as a priori principle that you're not allowed to develop abstract
theories. As he puts it, you're not allowed to develop theories of
internal representation or mental structure, to postulate mental
structures, which in this domain simply means you're not allowed to
have theories of a non-trivial character. Naturally, anyone who
insists on this doctrine — merely a form a mysticism — is never
going to get anywhere. And investigating the system as it develops
you find, not unexpectedly, that it simply has no principles that
one can put to the test. My criticism has nothing to do with the
relationship of structure and function. Skinner put forth no
account of either, as far as I can see, but merely developed a
terminology which he prefers to traditional "mentalistic" terminology, apparently because of highly misleading connotations that
vaguely suggest experimental procedures.

RIEBER: What we've been talking about so far has been the verbal signal system. Lets go on to the nonverbal system. How much of the nonverbal system is helping the verbal system grow in the beginning stages, and once it's gotten formulated, how do they reciprocally influence one another? That is to say.

III. Are the verbal and nonverbal signal systems interrelated?

CHOMSKY: Let me stress again that I don't have any doctrine on this matter; the facts are whatever they turn out to be. A second point I ought to stress is that I don't think there is really any serious evidence about this; all we can do for the moment is speculate, beyond certain fairly obvious remarks. There are certain obvious interconnections between the verbal and gestural systems. In fact it's enough to watch somebody talking to notice that — as I'm talking now — I'm gesturing all over the place — anybody who's observing these gestures would notice that they relate in all sorts of ways to the form and content of my utterance. For example, I stress something by a gesture, but even the phrasing — the intonation structure of the utterance — corresponds in quite obvious ways to things going on in the gestural system. They're in tandem, and some common source is obviously controlling them both; they're just too well correlated for anything else to be the case. Nevertheless, the system of gestures is very different in its underlying principles from the system of language. The system of gestures, in fact, seems to have very much the properties of what might be called "verbal gestures," for example, stress or pitch. If you consider the system of intonation in language — stress and pitch basically — you can immediately separate out two different components. On the one hand, there is a continuous component; that is, the loudness, the pitch peaks in my utterances can vary in principle over a continuous range, in whatever sense it makes to talk about continuous dimensions in the physical world. The more agitated I become, the more I want to pointedly emphasize something, the greater the stress and the higher the pitch will be at the end, again over a continuous range. So there is a continuous system which looks as though it has very much the properties of nonverbal gesture. If someone were observing me carefully, he might notice that my arms move more when the intonational peaks in my utterances are higher. There might be such a correlation. On the other hand, there is another element in the stress and pitch system that is radically different in character. There are significant respects in which the whole intonational contour of an utterance — it's stress patterns and pitch patterns — is closely related to the discrete hierarchical phrase structure, and internal word structure for that matter, that reflects the rules of English grammar. In the actual performance of language, these two systems interact. So, for example, the abstract phrase structure of the utterance that I'm now producing determines one of a discrete set of possible abstract pitch and stress patterns. But then some other kind of system interacts and spreads that over a continuous

range. I'm now talking on just the verbal side, and even here we
find, I think, quite different systems; one a system which is
really as much a part of the discrete grammar of English as is, say,
segmental phonology, words, structure, or syntactic phrase structure.
Similarly there is a gestural system that shows up in speech as well.
For example, it expresses itself in the range of intonation or
stress contours that somehow are constructed on the scaffolding that
derives from the rules of grammar.

RIEBER: Do you believe there is a grammar of gesture?

CHOMSKY: That's a very different question. I've been talking
not about sign language, but about the gestural system that is
associated with spoken language. Sign language undoubtedly has a
grammar as does spoken language, and in the actual use of sign
language, we surely will find the same kind of interaction of a
discrete grammatical system and a gestural system that we find in
spoken language.

Presumably there is a system, a set of principles, that determines the nature of the gestural system and the way in which it
interacts with the language system, but whether those principles
should be called a grammar is another question. I would think that
it is a dubious metaphor, because it leads one to expect commonality
of structure, and that is very much an open question. In fact, it
seems to me that there isn't likely to be much structure in common.
Even at the most rudimentary level the systems appear to diverge
radically. A system of principles that determines the nature of
some continuous system is going to be very different from a system
of principles that determines the nature of some discrete system.
And as we proceed, I think we will find more and more divergencies.
To a certain extent, at least, the gestural system is like a speed-
ometer; perhaps the degree of my commitment to what I am saying is
reflected in the extent to which my arm moves while I'm saying it.
This is almost like a recording device. There is undoubtedly much
more to continuous gesture than that, but there is at least that.
Now that's a property that doesn't appear at all in the discrete
system of recursive rules that determine the formal structure of
language, and that determine what I called the basic scaffolding on
which the stress and intonational contours are constructed. It may
be, incidentally, that sign language does make use of such properties.

RIEBER: Speaking of stress and rhythm, do you feel that the
study of stress contours etc. has any possibility of getting us
closer to the biological basis of the structure of language?

CHOMSKY: I would think that the study of any aspect of language
has a possibility of getting us to the biological structure.

RIEBER: Some may offer better bets than others.

CHOMSKY: I think they're just going to lead us to different aspects of the biological structure. For example, the study of abstract syntax or abstract phonology leads to certain aspects of the biological structure of language, that is, to crucial and intrinsic elements of cognition. The study of stress and intonational contours — as I mentioned, we have to separate the components of those, one of them being very much like abstract syntax and phonology, but the other one, a continuous system which has at least some of the properties of a recording device — that may tell us something about other aspects of the biological basis for human language — for example, about rhythm and symmetry and properties of serial behavior, the sort of thing that Lashley talked about years ago, all undoubtedly other aspects of our biological nature.

But I would still want to resist what is a very common assumption, and I think one that is totally wrong, namely that the study of the abstract structure of language can't tell us anything about what is sometimes called "psychological reality" or biological nature. On the contrary, it is precisely telling us about psychological reality in the only meaningful sense of that word, and also about our biological nature, namely — ultimately — the set of genetically determined principles that provide the basis for the growth and development of these specific capacities.

RIEBER: Why do you think that mistake has been made?

CHOMSKY: I think the mistake has a curious history, and maybe the easiest way to explain would be to talk a little bit about the history. Maybe the first use of the phrase "psychological reality" is in Edward Sapir's paper in, I think, 1933 on the psychological reality of the phoneme, which has become a sort of locus classicus for this discussion. (Sapir, 1933). Sapir, in this paper, tried to show that the reactions of his informants, in American Indian languages, provide evidence that the phonemic analyses that he was proposing for these languages were psychologically real.

RIEBER: Meaning what?

CHOMSKY: What did he mean by that? That's the interesting question. Let's reconstruct what Sapir was doing — or intimated that he was doing. He was investigating the data of a language — the phonetic data of the language — and he proposed a rather abstract phonological structure that he claimed underlies the range of phonetic phenomena that he studied. The empirical justification for the postulated abstract phonological structure was simply that if you assumed it, then you could explain many of the phonetic facts, you could show that the phonetic facts were not just a random array of disorder, but that in fact they reflected some simple

principles; there were interesting abstract principles from which
a range of phenomena follow. Notice that Sapir did not take that to
be an argument for psychological reality. That is, he did not conclude from the fact that he was able to construct an abstract theory
of, say, Southern Paiute phonology on the basis of which a variety
of facts could be elegantly explained — he did not take that as a
demonstration of psychological reality for the underlying phonological
theory. Rather, he clearly felt that in order to demonstrate
psychological reality he needed some other kind of evidence; for
example, evidence that under some conditions his American Indian
informant seemed to be hearing something that was not physically
present, and other behavior of that sort. Implicit in Sapir's
approach was the assumption that there are two kinds of evidence in
this field. There is the kind of evidence provided by the phonetic
data themselves — these provide evidence for the correctness of the
phonological analysis. And there's another kind of evidence, namely
behavioral evidence of some different sort, which is evidence for
the psychological reality of that phonological analysis. As the
discussion of psychological reality has proceeded since that time,
this assumption has been held constant. I don't want to run through
the whole history; but coming right up to the present, the same
distinction is quite common. If you look at the latest issue of a
journal with an article on psychological reality, you will find
almost invariably that the question raised is: what is the evidence
for the psychological reality of some linguistic construction? A
linguist proposes some principle or structure for English, say,
such-and-such a phonological system or condition on syntactic rules,
or whatever. Then someone comes along and says, "all right, that's
very interesting; but what's the evidence for the psychological
reality of the systems and principles that you've postulated?" The
evidence is supposed to come from an experiment in which a subject
is pushing buttons or something like that. Now again the presuppo-
sition is that the data available to us fall into two categories.
There are the data that come from experiments and bear on psychological reality; and there are the data provided by, let's say,
informant judgments or language use itself which don't bear on
psychological reality, but on something else. But this distinction
is senseless.

RIEBER: Some people, I think, have raised the question of
"psychological reality" on the basis that literature sometimes refers
to something as having a psychological reality that was generated
by the mind of the writer of the article.

CHOMSKY: That's right.

RIEBER: And only by the mind of the writer of the article.

CHOMSKY: True enough, but that kind of criticism is quite
independent of the senseless distinction I have been discussing.

One can do a bad job of constructing theories on the basis of
evidence derived from button-pushing, informant judgment, electrodes
in the brain, or whatever. What I would like to suggest is the
following, going back to Sapir. He was looking at the phonetic data
from a certain American Indian language and was able to show that if
he assumed a certain abstract phonological structure with rules of
various kinds, he could account for properties of these data. He
could explain some of the facts of the language. That investigation
in itself was an investigation of psychological reality in the only
meaningful sense of the term. That is, he was showing that if we
take his phonological theory to be a theory about the mind — that
is, if we adapt the standard "realist" assumptions of the natural
sciences — then we conclude that in proposing this phonological
theory he was saying something about the mental organization of the
speakers of the language, namely that their knowledge and use of
their language involved certain types of mental representations and
not others — ultimately, certain physical structures and processes
and not others differently characterized. That is, he was making a
claim about psychological reality, and he had evidence for it. The
evidence was that his hypothesis would explain some facts. And that
is the only sense in which there ever is evidence to support a truth-
claim about reality — physical or psychological. In fact, the so-
called "psychological evidence," the behavioral evidence that Sapir
adduced, was arguably weaker than the so-called "linguistic evidence"
adduced with regard to the correctness of the postulated abstract
theory. But he would not have written the article the other way
around, that is, first noting his informant's reactions (the "psychological evidence"), then postulating a phonological theory to account
for these reactions, and then appealing to the explanatory power of
this phonological theory as evidence for its "psychological reality,"
that is, its truth. The same is true if we move to the present.
Suppose that a linguist today proposes some abstract principle of
grammar, or some constraint on the operation of rules, and suppose
he argues for that principle on the basis of a demonstration, which
let us assume to be a very convincing demonstration so that we don't
run into the question of accuracy — we'll just look at the logic
of the situation; suppose he can give a very convincing demonstration
that by assuming that abstract principle, let's say governing the
manner of application and the nature of rules, he can explain some
very strange phenomena about our explicit and manifest knowledge.
The linguist has thereby provided evidence for the psychological
reality of that abstract principle in the only sense in which one
can provide evidence for the "reality" of a theoretical construction,
i.e., for its truth. The objection that you cite, namely, how do
you know it's not just the invention of a theorist, can be answered
only in one way; by considering how well the theory explains the
evidence and how significant the evidence is. To persist with this
objection in the face of a convincing explanation of interesting
facts, that is, to ask for some other kind of justification, would
be simply perverse. To see that, we can transfer the whole

discussion over to the physical sciences. Suppose, for example, someone....

RIEBER: I think I understand what you mean, but I would like your reaction to this, because I think you're simply using the word differently. People to say that. I would interpret their use of the word "psychological reality" to mean that it's only real if enough people engage in it, and one person's engaging in it might simply be idiosyncratic, and therefore may be psychologically real to that individual, but not generalizable as a psychologically real principle.

CHOMSKY: I don't believe that this is the way the issue is perceived, but let's take a look at this question: the difference   · between what idiosyncratic and what is common to some group. Fine. How do we investigate that. Well, let's keep within the range of what is called, in what seems to me a rather misleading locution, "linguistic evidence." So, let's suppose that I'm investigating the speech of some speaker — let's say, myself — and I find that there is a strange array of acceptable and unacceptable utterances. Suppose I'm considering interrogative expressions. I find that some are well-informed (for example, "who do you think won the game") while others are not (for example, "who did you ask what game won," meaning: "who is the person x such that you asked what game x won"). Suppose now I find that I can explain the array of possible and impossible questions by assuming some abstract principles that constrains the grammar. Then somebody comes along and says, how do you know that's not idiosyncratic. We know how to find out: I look at the next person and see whether he has a comparable array of possible and unacceptable interrogative expressions and a comparable system. Suppose I find that I can explain that person's array of acceptable and unacceptable utterances by the same principle, and so on. Suppose I go and find that the same principle also enters into explanations for other phenomena in this language or other languages. All of this is what is called "linguistic evidence." Let's now assume the usage you suggest. Then the first investigation of one speaker provides evidence for the psychological reality of that abstract principle for that speaker — that is, evidence supporting the theory incorporating this principle, or in other words, evidence supporting the hypothesis that the theory and the principle are true, for this speaker. The question you raise is whether the result generalizes; notice that it is not a question about psychological reality, rather it is a question about the generality of a certain conclusion about psychological reality.

RIEBER: Most people who have been objecting to the use of that term have been objecting to that meaning.

CHOMSKY: No, that's not correct. I'm sure that's not correct. The argument is not that the results do not generalize. The people who have been raising questions about 'the psychological reality of linguistic constructions" would have said that the evidence provided for the first speaker doesn't support a claim of psychological reality for that speaker, and would not matter how extensive and compelling that evidence is; it is somehow "the wrong kind of evidence." The so-called "linguistic evidence" can, in principle, only establish that the principle in question suffices to provide explanations, but somehow does not bear on this mysterious quality of "psychological reality." A demonstration of psychological reality requires evidence about reaction time or something of that sort. That is, it requires what is called "psychological evidence."

RIEBER: But surely psychological evidence would be observing behavior that's common to enough people to make it psychological evidence.

CHOMSKY: I don't see that. We can perfectly well have so-called "psychological evidence" about a particular person. There are two quite different issues here. The first is whether we have a correct theory for the individual in question; the second is whether the correct theory for the individual in question happens to be similar in interesting respects to the correct theory for some other individual. These are different questions.

RIEBER: Individual differences as opposed to generalized differences.

CHOMSKY: Fine. But the whole discussion of psychological reality takes place on a different dimension. It has nothing to do with individual differences and shared group properties. Let me make it concrete. Suppose the subjacency principle to account for a certain informant's judgments about what is and what is not a properly-formed question, as in the examples I just mentioned. Without going into details, this principle holds that mental computations have to be "locul" in a well-defined sense, and it does in fact provide an explanation from the phenomena I haven't shown anything about "psychological reality" for this person; I've only mentioned, along with much else, within a certain theory of grammar. Now the standard response would be that which explains what he does. To show "psychological reality," one would have to do an experiment involving reaction time, etc. Suppose I then proceed to show that for the next person I study the same principle of subjacency accounts for what that person is doing, and for the next person. Suppose the result extends to other phenomena and other languages. The response would still be: you haven't yet given any evidence for "psychological reality;" you've only shown that you have a simple and elegant theory that accounts for a lot of facts, and who says that nature is simple. In contrast, even the weakest evidence concerning reaction time, etc., is held to bear on "psychological reality." The evidence falls into two different logical categories: some evidence is labelled "for explanatory theories;" other evidence is labelled "for psychological reality." That is the tacit assumption that is pervasive in the literature all the way back to Sapir. Again I think that one can see what is wrong in the whole debate by transferring it over to the physical sciences, and trying to imagine a comparable situation. Imagine that some astrophysicists have developed a theory about what is happening in the interior of the sun on the basis of observations of light emitted from the solar periphery. Suppose they analyze the light that is emitted and they develop some kind of complicated theory about fusion, and so on, and then suppose someone comes along and says, "Well, that's very interesting, but how do you know you've established "physical reality?" What's your evidence that the structures, entities, processes and principles that you have postulated have the property of physical reality?" What could the scientists respond? They could only say, "We've already given you evidence that justifies our claim concerning physical reality, namely, it is that if we assume these entities, etc., we can explain the properties of the light emitted from the solar periphery." And then suppose the interlocutor says, "Well, that's all very interesting. I agree that you have a simple explanatory theory, but how do you know that what you have assumed is real? Perhaps the light emissions result from the mischievious acts of a Cartesian demon. The physicists could only respond, "we told you what we think is real and why. We'll be glad to search for more evidence, but since your objection does not rest on the inadequacy of evidence that won't help. Furthermore, you have not presented any alternative explanatory theory for consideration." We have an impasse.

In fact such discussions don't take place in the physical sciences. The reason is that certain canons of rationality are assumed, one of them being that a claim to have demonstrated "physical reality" is nothing more than a claim to have developed an intelligible, powerful explanatory theory dealing with some range of significant phenomena. The phenomena that are being explained are what provide the evidence for the correctness, the truth, the "physical reality" if you like, of the constructions of the theory. If we were to adopt these canons of rationality in the human sciences, we would see at once that the whole discussion of "psychological reality" is just off the wall. To the extent that Sapir or anyone has convincing "linguistic evidence" for a theory that postulates some abstract structure or process, to exactly that extent he has provided evidence for the truth of that theory, that is, for the "psychological reality" of its constructs, in the only meaningful sense of the term.

RIEBER: So what you're saying, if I understand you correctly, is that the arguments about psychological reality boil down to one person simply saying that your truth ain't my truth.

CHOMSKY: What it boils down to, I think, is that quite irrational attitudes often prevail within the human sciences. For example, the assumption I have already mentioned that evidence comes labelled in one of two categories. Some come with the label, "I bear on psychological reality" — namely, studies of reaction time, etc. Other evidence comes with the label, "I only bear on the correctness of theories" — for example, evidence about the distribution of phones, about well-formedness of sentences, etc. It is not a matter of "my truth versus your truth;" rather of rationality versus irrationality. Recall that the issue is not the quality of the evidence or its relevance to selecting among theories, or the depth or explanatory force of the theories. The most insignificant result about reaction times is supposed to bear on "psychological reality" in a way in which even the strongest and most varied "linguistic evidence" in principle cannot. It's as if someone came to the physicist and said, "your evidence about the sun only has to do with light being emitted from the solar periphery, and I don't call that evidence about 'reality.' For me, evidence about 'reality' is limited to experiments in a laboratory placed inside the sun where you actually observe hydrogen becoming helium, and so on." That's obviously absurd. What I think is remarkable about our disciplines, right up to the present, is that the basic approach of the natural sciences is so commonly rejected. I believe, frankly, that this is one reason why so much of psychology never gets anywhere: it refuses to accept the canons of rationality that have been standard in the natural sciences for centuries. The a priori objection to theoretical constructions that go beyond some arbitrary level of complexity and abstractness is one such example. One might read the whole curious history of behaviorism as a series of variations on this theme. And the debate about psychological reality is another case in point. If someone were to claim, let's say, that he had evidence for the psychological reality of the subjacency principle, that he could use it to explain such-and-such facts about the form and interpretation of linguistic expressions, the response would not be; "your evidence isn't strong enough." That would be a rational response. Somebody could say, that's interesting, but I don't think the evidence is very strong, and the theory seems rather shallow. That's a rational response, perhaps even the correct response. But that's not the response that you hear. The response is....

RIEBER: When they say it's not strong enough, did they mean that they did agree in principle with your basic method?

CHOMSKY: No that's not true.

RIEBER: Well perhaps they didn't agree with the way you got there.

CHOMSKY: No, I don't think that's quite it either. What happens, I think, is that experiments involving memory or reaction

time, for example, are regarded as providing evidence for "psychological reality," whereas evidence of the so-called "linguistic"
type would be regarded as in principle providing no evidence at all
about psychological reality. So it's not that the linguistic
evidence is not too compelling. Rather, it's that it's evidence of
the wrong type, and therefore no matter how much more of that sort
of evidence you accumulate, the same kind of critique would be given.
Now that's just irrational, as soon as one begins to analyse it, the
whole long debate makes no sense from the outset.

IV. *How can one best deal with the issue of nature versus nurture
    in our attempts to unravel the basic issues in the field of
    language and cognition?*

   (a) *Of what importance is the biological basis of language
       perception and production?*

   (b) *Of what importance is the study of individuals who suffer
       from pathological conditions of language and thought?*

RIEBER: I would like to get your reaction to something specific.
People have accused you of neglecting the importance of the environment in your notion of the structure of language and the theory of
language, and as I recall you have repeatedly denied this.

CHOMSKY: Let me begin by saying something that I hope is
uncontroversial. Namely, there is something characteristic of the
human species — there is some species-specific property, some part
of the human biological endowment that contributes to the growth of
language in the mind. That is, language doesn't grow in a rock or
in a bird under comparable conditions of stimulation. That's
obvious, I hope. So therefore, there is something about the human
mind that plays a role in determining that knowledge of language
grows, develops in that mind. A second point that is equally
obvious is that the way in which language grows in the mind is going
to be affected by the nature of the outside environment; that is,
if we're growing up in the United States, we'll learn to speak
English and if we're growing up in some parts of East Africa, we'll
learn to speak Swahili. That's again obvious. So what's clear is
that there is some biological capacity which differentiates us from
rocks and birds and apes and so on; it plainly isn't just a sensory
capacity, because we can easily translate language into some other
sensory modality accessible to birds or apes and the same observation
will hold. So there is some mental characteristic, if you like —
something about our nature which reflects itself in the structure
and growth of a particular mental organ and that constitutes the
intrinsic, innate contribution to the growth of language. And there
are also environmental factors, which have both a triggering effect
and a shaping effect on the growth of this intrinsically determined
"mental organ." It is, incidentally, important to distinguish the

triggering and the shaping effect. Certain conditions may be
required for a given system to function and develop, even though
they do not shape its development; other conditions may determine
how the system functions and develops. Consider for example the
development of the mammalian visual system. It has reported that
mother-neonate contact is a prerequisite for the development of
normal depth perception in sheep, for example. Suppose that this
is the case. Then we would conclude that some kind of social interaction has a triggering effect on the growth and functioning of a
biologically determined system, but not (at least, not necessarily)
that it shapes this growth and function. In contrast, the distribution of horizontal and vertical lines in the visual field appears
to shape the growth of the mammalian visual system. It may not be
easy to separate out the strands, but the conceptual distinction
is important. Plainly, neither mother-neonate contact with its
presumed triggering effect or distribution of lines in the visual
field with its apparent shaping effect is going to determine that
the visual system will be that of a cat and not a rabbit or a bee.
But the triggering conditions must be fulfilled for the system to
develop or function in a certain way and the shaping conditions will
play a role in specifiying and articulating that growth and function.
Similarly in the case of language, it may be that certain types of
social interaction play a triggering role and there is no doubt that
environmental factors play a shaping role.

So there is an intrinsic, genetically determined factor in
language growth; the term "universal grammar," as I've already
mentioned, is often used for the theory that attempts to characterise
one fundamental component of this aspect of the genotype. And there
are environmental factors of several sorts that trigger and shape
language growth, as the biologically-given capacity grows and matures
in the early years of life. The problem is, then, to tease out these
distinct contributions. That they both exist is beyond question,
at least among rational people. The problem is to separate and
identify them (and furthermore, to distinguish triggering and shaping
factors, among the environmental factors). Now turning to your
question, it is quite possible that in my own efforts to separate
these factors I've tended to slight the environmental factors, and
it is, in my opinion, even more likely that I've tended to underestimate the innate endowment, because of an inadequate and superficial understanding of univeral grammar. But that is a question
of fact — an interesting and very important question of fact. To
show that I have not given enough weight to the environment, one
would have to demonstrate that in the particular proposals I've
made, where I've tried to deal with certain phenomena in terms of
principles of universal grammar, in fact these phenomena should be
explained, let's say as a reflection of some environmental factor.
To be concrete, consider again the example we've already discussed
briefly, namely, the rule of question-formation in English. To
pick standard examples, we know that the interrogative expressions

"who do you think will win the game" or "what do you believe that
John told Mary that Bill saw" are properly formed in a way in which
"who do you think that will win the game" or "who did you ask what
game will win" or "who do you believe the claim that John saw" are
not. I've tried to explain such facts as these on the basis of
principles of universal grammar, say the subjacency principle which
I've already mentioned. Now someone else might come along and say,
no, these are just idiosyncratic properties reflecting environmental
factors. You tried to say the "bad" sentences and your mother
slapped you on the wrist. Or something like that. That's how you
came to make the distinction. Well, there's a factual question here,
obviously.

RIEBER: Maybe you just never heard them.

CHOMSKY: Well the fact that you never heard the sentences you
know to be improperly formed doesn't help, because it is also most
unlikely that you have heard the ones you know to be properly formed,
or anything resembling them. You say many things you've never heard,
all the time. For example, it is unlikely that you or I have even
heard anybody say, "who did Mary tell Sam that Tom was likely to
see." We've never heard that before, and quite possibly never heard
an instance of that category sequence before, but we know that that's
a well-formed sentence. So the fact that I didn't hear the improper
sentence explains nothing, because among the things that I never
heard, some of them I recognize as well-formed sentences and give an
interpretation to, and others I recognize as not well-formed
sentences though often I know perfectly well what meaning they would
have, were they properly formed. All of this takes us back to the
most elementary property of language, its discrete infinity, from
which we see at once that only a trivial sub-part has ever been
heard, and that sub-part we cannot possibly remember. That is, no
one can recall whether or not he has heard a particular sentence or
sentence type, with trivial exceptions. In order to show that these
phenomena reflect something about the environment, one would have to
show something about the specific training or something of that sort.
Evidence would have to be produced to show that these phenomena are
a reflection of the environment. If some such explanation could be
produced, if, for example, some account can be produced of the
phenomena concerning the rule of question-formation on the basis of
environmental factors, I'd certainly want to look at it. What we
find, however, is something totally different. Namely, people argue
that environmental factors are critical but without offering any
account of the facts in question in terms of such alleged factors.
And as long as they don't produce any moderately plausible account
in terms of presumed environmental factors, all I can say is that
they're not holding my attention. It is not very interesting if
somebody claims that something is the result of the environment or
an act of God or electrical storms in the vicinity, or whatever, if
they don't provide some explanatory scheme that can at least be
investigated.

RIEBER: What I would like to know is what specifically, would you use to show how the environment does play a role in the acquisition of language.

CHOMSKY: It's easy enough to find a concrete example. The fact that I call this thing a table instead of a sulxan, which I'd say if I'd learned Hebrew, plainly reflects the fact that I grew up in the United States and not in Israel.

RIEBER: Yes, but what about within a particular language itself?

CHOMSKY: Well, there are things which are certainly a reflection of environment. The example I just mentioned, for one, or the fact that the detailed phonetics of my speech happens to be very much like, I'm sure, a small group of people who were around me in my childhood. Mostly my peers rather than my parents. That fact undoubtedly relates to environmental factors in the growth of language.

RIEBER: You might slip in a little Philadelphia accent every once in a while, like I do.

CHOMSKY: All I have to do is listen to myself on a tape recorder to see that it's not so little, even though I haven't lived there for over twenty-five years. But it seems to be the case that a child will develop the detailed phonetic characteristics of his peers, and that these tend to persist substantially after adolescence. So, for example, the child of immigrant parents will speak like his schoolmates, and will do so to a fantastic degree of fineness of reproduction, far beyond anything required for communicative efficiency or the like. For example, if I had spoken with a slightly different phonetics, nobody would have even noticed it, but the point is there's something about us that makes us mimic to an incredible degree of refinement properties of the phonetic environment in which we live at an early stage of childhood. That's a striking example of the effect of the environment on the development of speech, within a particular language. There are many others, of course, at every level of language structure and use of language.

RIEBER: You know the examples that the anthropologists have used for years about differences between Navaho and English, that Navaho and Hopi have a different structural quality to them that seems to center very much around the verb rather than the noun. Would you consider that to be a function of environment.

CHOMSKY: First I would want to establish the facts. It's only been in the last few years that there have been investigations of Navaho and Hopi, in particular, of a sufficient level of depth for such questions to be seriously raised. In fact there's been a qualitative advance in the nature of linguistic research into Navaho

and Hopi, those two cases in particular, because for the first time
native Americans for whom these are the native languages have been
adequately trained in linguistics, largely by my colleague Ken Hale
at MIT, so that they can begin to investigate their languages the
way we investigate English. This has led to remarkable advances, I
believe, in the level of the research that's being done, so that now
perhaps one can begin for the first time to raise the kinds of
questions to which people have given all sorts of dubious answers
in the past. I'm not convinced that anything of the sort you suggest
can as yet be substantiated. True, those languages differ from, say,
English in many different respects, and these undoubtedly....

    RIEBER: Let's just assume that if you take a Navaho speaker
and an American speaker and you translate Navaho into English, but
you do it and the American speaker says, I'm dying, and the Navaho
speaker says, death is taking place with me. The Navahos seem to
utter things that exemplify their view of themselves in the world
where action is at the center of things rather than nouns.

    CHOMSKY: I don't understand what that means. English
certainly....

    RIEBER: If I say death is taking place with me instead of I
am dying, what is the difference between the two statements.

    CHOMSKY: Well, if I say I am dying, dying is not an action
anyway. For nobody, neither the Navaho nor us, is dying an action,
I would think. And certainly English grammar is crucially based on
verb structure and relations of nominal and other categories to
verbs, and on what have been called "thematic relations" between
noun phrases and verbs, and so on. May be it will turn out that
there is some difference between Navaho and English in this respect,
but I'd like to see the evidence before,.... I'd like to see a
coherent question.

    RIEBER: Well, the difference between those two utterances:
would they primarily be a difference of biology or environment?

    CHOMSKY: What differences there may be are obviously environ-
mental. That is, I don't say the sentence in Navaho, and the Navaho
doesn't say the sentence in English, but I assume that there is no
relevant distinction in genotype. We obey the same principles of
universal grammar.

    RIEBER: So there's something in the environment that precipi-
tated this different structure.

    CHOMSKY: If there is one. But that's even true at the level
of the sounds we produce. The sounds we produce are different, the
words are different, their organization is different, and so on.

You're raising the question of whether the conceptual structures associated with those utterances are different, and as to that, I simply think that we don't know.

RIEBER: There were two questions there. There was the one you first mentioned, and there was the other, namely, does something in the environment produce the difference that we notice as a difference. Are you saying may be there really isn't a difference that makes a difference?

CHOMSKY: At the level of conceptual structure? First we have to see if at the level of conceptual structure there is a difference. If there is then it will be because of the environment. What else could it be? I don't think that you and I are genetically different from the Navaho speaker in any relevant respect. So in fact where-ever we can find a difference of phonetic or synthactic or conceptual structure, we will naturally assume that it is somehow related to environmental factors.

RIEBER: Wouldn't it be possible that a pure Navaho that was born only out of Navaho stock may be inheriting some kind of structural difference for his language.

CHOMSKY: It's certainly a logical possibility, but I don't think anyone takes it very seriously. Of course it's never been studied in a systematic way, but the evidence we have certainly suggests that, say, if I were to adopt a Navaho child, that child would grow up speaking English as if he were my own child. That is, there is no evidence that I know of for the differentiation of the human species into language types. There are people who argue that: Darlington, for instance, if I remember correctly. But I doubt that anyone takes that very seriously.

RIEBER; It's not a point of view that you would take, or is it?

CHOMSKY: It is conceivable. It wouldn't even terribly surprise me, nor would it be particularly interesting as far as I can see. There are other respects in which human beings differ from one another genetically — height, weight, skin color, hair length, and all sorts of things — and it's conceivable that they also differ in some marginal respect with regard to the mental organ of language. But if there is such a difference at all, I would assume that it's at such a remote periphery that to investigate it would be completely pointless at the present.

RIEBER: Some people have been disturbed with your use of the word "organ of language." In terms of structure, they feel that it's rather simplistic to say that language is an organ, like the heart or the liver, and that it's a misrepresentation of a very dynamic, complex system.

CHOMSKY: That's a curious argument. Suppose, in fact, that
language is, as such critics assume, an extremely complex system —
let's assume for the sake of discussion that the language system is
far more complex than, say, the heart or the visual system. We then
notice something else: this highly complex system, which we're
assuming, say, to be far beyond other physical systems in complexity,
nevertheless develops in an essentially uniform way, across
individuals. You and I can converse perfectly well about some topic
we've never discussed before, which presumably means that this
marvellously intricate system in your brain has developed in more or
less the same way that it has developed in my brain. So what we are
now considering is the following assumption, or mixture of assumption
and fact: (1) that the system of language that develops is very
complex, far beyond the physical organs; (2) what is plainly a fact,
namely, that it's essentially uniform over a significant range among
individuals. Now the conclusion that follows from those assumptions
is that the basic properties of the whole system are genetically
determined. The structural properties and functions of this system
and its interactions with other cognitive structures must be largely
intrinsically determined, if in fact systems of remarkable complexity
and intricacy develop in an essentially uniform way in an environment
that is plainly not articulated and differentiated in anything like
sufficient detail to fix these specific properties. That would seem
an unavoidable consequence if indeed we assume, with the critics you
mention, that the resulting system is one of a very high order of
complexity and specific structure. But that is simply to say that
we have reached the conclusion that it is quite appropriate to regard
the "language faculty" as in effect a "mental organ," in the sense
that I suggested; that is, to assume that it is genetically determined in considerable and specific detail as one component of the
mind, neurally represented in some as yet unknown fashion. There is
no other way to account for the high degree of intricate, specific
structure and uniformity of growth of the system.

I think it can be a useful corrective for fields like psychology
and linguistics to transfer the kinds of questions that they raise
over to the domain of the physical sciences, because very often when
you do that you see that the questions are badly formulated. I
think that this is a case in point. Suppose someone were to come
along and say, look, I don't believe that the development of the
heart or the circulatory system or the visual system — I don't
believe that any of these things are genetically determined. I
think they are learned by the embryo; that is, the embryo tries all
sorts of different things and finds that the circulatory system seems
to work out best, or perhaps there is some environmental factor that
we don't know about yet that reinforces the random experiments of
the developing embryo, determining by reinforcement that it develops
a heart instead of some other system; that's how the organism
develops a heart. And that's why the human embryo grows arms instead
of wings. It's a reflection of the embryological environment. The

embryo tries out a lot of possibilities and arms seem to work out
better than wings, or something like that. If such a proposal were
made, people wouldn't even bother to ridicule it. Let's take an
example from post-natal development; let's take, say, onset of
puberty. Suppose someone comes along and says, I think that people
learned that, if they don't try to, or try not to reach sexual
maturity, then their friends laugh at them and their parents punish
them; and if they try to, they get rewarded. It's just a matter of
copying other people who have gone through puberty. Again, such
suggestions would not even be an object of ridicule. What everybody
assumes without even discussing it is that all the things that I've
just described are genetically determined. But let's ask why these
suggestions are so ridiculous. That's an interesting question. It's
not because we know the answer to the question how pre-natal growth
takes place. Nobody knows much about that. Nobody can tell you
what in the genes determines the growth of organs or, say, the onset
of puberty. Still, it's taken for granted that it is a genetically
determined maturational process in all these cases. Why? Well, only
because of the high degree of specificity and uniformity of the
process or the result of the process — there's such a qualitative
gap between that degree of specificity and uniformity on the one hand
and the environmental stimulation on the other that it's inconceivable that these developments are reflecting some property of the
environment. Let's go back now and look at the language case.
Notice that on your own assumption the same conclusion holds
a fortiori, because in fact what is assumed by the critics you cite
is that the language system is even more complex than any of the
physical organs which are taken to be determined by genetic endowment.
And, of course, the development of this immensely complex system is
quite uniform among people. So there is a uniform development to
an even more complex system, with no apparent possibility, so far as
we know, of relating it to environmental factors.

RIEBER: I think that when you talk about the liver and heart,
there doesn't seem to be a by-product of the interface between, say,
mental and somatic life. You get such things as language, you get
a structure and a process which is a by-product of the interface
between mental and physical life.

CHOMSKY: But that comes back to my original point. Why should
we abandon normal canons of rationality when we turn to the study of
the mind? It's certainly true that the study of the mind has to do
with different systems than in the conventional study of the body.
But the question I'm asking is why should we abandon the approach
we take for granted in studying the body when we turn to the study
of the mind. What you're saying is that, look, this has to do with
the mind, therefore it works differently. But that's not answering
the question.

RIEBER: No, I said it has to do with the relationship between
the body and the mind.

CHOMSKY: Okay, so why should we abandon normal canons of rationality when we talk about the relationship of the body and mind, — bearing in mind, again, that the study of mind is a study of a very poorly understood physical system, conducted at an appropriate level of abstraction.

RIEBER: I don't think you should.

CHOMSKY: Well, if we don't; then the very same considerations that lead us to take for granted that there is a genetically deter- mined process of maturation in the course of physical organ growth will lead us to assume a fortiori that the same is true of mental organ growth. That turns out to be not only a reasonable approach, but also a successful one — the only successful one, to my knowledge.

RIEBER: But the point I'm trying to make, and I'd like your reaction to is that obviously the mind can influence the body, and the body can influence the mind. Nobody in his right mind would think that the mind can in its structural development can influence the structure of the heart, or the structure of the liver.

CHOMSKY: That's absolutely untrue. Take the study of psycho- somatic medicine.

RIEBER: Well, you're just altering the structure. You are born with the structure of the heart.

CHOMSKY: You're born with the structure of language. I know of no reason to believe that there is any fundamental difference in the respects in which the human embryo has at the earliest stage the potential structure of the heart on the one hand, and the potential structure of language on the other.

RIEBER: But it doesn't unfold in language until the first year of life. You can look at the heart when it comes out. You can see its structure.

CHOMSKY: That's why I gave the example of puberty. There is plenty of post-natal physical development, evidently; in fact there is a lot of neural maturation of the brain that takes place well after birth in humans particularly. Does anybody doubt that the dendritic growth that's going on from ages two to four is genetically determined? Do they think it's a reflection of the environment? In fact, take the study of the maturation that takes place in the visual system after birth. Or take even dramatic cases of genetically determined maturation such as puberty, for instance; or for that matter, death, which takes place long after birth, but is genetically determined. We are determined to be the kind of organism that will die after so many years. Obviously physical growth takes place after birth; nobody thinks it's learned. No one thinks that children are reinforced to grow until age seventeen or thereabouts, and then they're not reinforced any more, so they stop growing. That's absurd. There's no specific moment — say, birth — at which qualitatively different things necessarily begin to happen. Many aspects of our physical development take place in a genetically determined fashion well after birth, of course, triggered and shaped in some manner by environmental factors — as is true of embryological development as well. Onset of puberty, for example, seems to vary with nutritional level over a considerable range, so is conditioned by environmental factors. But does anybody get confused about that and think that we learn to undergo puberty? Of course not. As far as I can see, as far as we have evidence at least....

RIEBER: You learn to cope with it.

CHOMSKY: But my point, to get back, is this. On the very assumption that you proposed — namely that the language system is far more complex than the obvious physical systems of the body, which may or may not be true — but if it is true then a fortiori you're led to the assumption that this is a case of strongly genetically determined maturation and specific development in a specific direction.

V.   *Of what importance is the current research in comparative psycholinguistics (recent attempts to train chimpanzees and/or apes via sign language or any other method)?*

CHOMSKY: Investigations that have been carried out so far I think are intriguing. Some of them — Premack's, for example — seem quite interesting. They tell us something about chimpanzee intelligence. As far as language is concerned, what this work has so far shown is, I think, about what anybody would have predicted in advance. Namely, as far as we know, even the most rudimentary characteristics of human language are completely beyond the capacities of apes that otherwise share many of the cognitive capacities of humans. At least that's the result of the work so far reported. For example, take the properties that I mentioned before when I was beginning to list the most elementary properties of language, for example, the fact that language involves a discrete infinity of utterances based on recursive rules involving phrases, building more complex phrases by recursive embedding of various structures, and so on. As I mentioned these are the most superficial and rudimentary properties of human language, and there seems to be nothing even remotely analogous in the systems that are laboriously imposed on apes. That's exactly what we should expect, I think. Why should we expect it? Because, if it turned out, contrary to what has so far been shown, if it turned out that apes really did have something like a capacity for human language, we would be faced with a kind of biological paradox. We would be faced with something analogous to, say, the discovery on a previously unexplored island

that there is a species of bird with all the mechanisms for flight
that has never though of flying, until somebody comes along and
trains it and says, look, you can fly. That's not impossible, but
it's so unlikely that nobdy would take the possibility very
seriously. Now of course there are capacities that are never
realized; for example, take the number capacity. That's a genetically determined capacity, no doubt, but it was never realized in
human life until long after human evolution was essentially
completed. So that part is not surprising. What would be quite
surprising, however, is the following: suppose that an organism has
a certain capacity and suppose that circumstances exist in normal
life for that capacity to be used. And suppose furthermore that
exercise of that capacity would confer enormous selectional advant-
ages. And suppose finally that the capacity is never put to use.
That would be a very strange phenomenon. I would be surprised if
there were examples of that in natural history or in biological
evolution. I think any biologist would be amazed to discover anything of the sort. But that's what people who are working with apes
somehow — a lot of them, not all of them — seem to believe to be
true. And while you can't rule out a priori, it seems to me quite
a long shot, a very exotic belief, and certainly one for which no
evidence has been forthcoming. So I would tend to dismiss it as —
it seems to me... Tom Sebeok once described it as an example of the
pathetic fallacy, the long-standing tendency to invest nature with
human properties. I suppose it's another case of that. It seems
to me that this kind of investigation may seem perfectly good sense
as a technique for learning something about the intellectual
capacities of apes, although whether this is the best way of
pursuing that question is perhaps open to doubt. One might find
much more substantial manifestations of ape intelligence by studying
what they do naturally, rather than training them in tasks that are
vaguely analogous to the early manifestations of certain human
capacities. Just as it would be a questionable research strategy
in the study of human intelligence to try to get human children to
behave like apes. One might learn something, but it doesn't seem
obvious that this is the most reasonable way to approach the problem
of investigating the capacities of a particular species. In fact,
it's for this reason that it seems to me that Premack's work has
been of considerable interest. He's not just trying to make the
apes behave as though they're funny-looking people, but rather to
investigate their intellectual capacities in a straightforward way.
There's nothing wrong with that, in fact, it is a very significant
line of research. And it seems to me, to repear, that in regard to
language, what has so far been found and what I anticipate will be
found is about what you'd expect, that apes lack the rudiments of
anything comparable to human language, at least in any domain in
which anything is known about human language — and, evidently, the
significance of analogies, dubious at best, is essentially nil outside of such domains. Similarly you may get humanbeings to jump
farther and farther, but they're never going to fly.

RIEBER: What are the most important and promising applications of research in the psychology of language and cognition? For example, in therapy, in teaching, etc.

CHOMSKY: My general feeling is that it's practitioners — therapists, teachers and so on who will have to explore these questions. It would be terribly presumptuous of me even to suggest anything. Because I have no experience, I have no particular knowledge about these matters. It would be particularly inappropriate for me to venture off-the-cuff comments or proposals because the questions are not academic but have important human consequences. I have opinions, of course, and sometimes voice them, but they do not derive from any special knowledge that I may have.

VII *Do you feel that the field of language and cognition is, as some believe, in a state of transition searching for a new theory or paradigm? If so, what kind of theory do you believe will emerge or is at present emerging?*

CHOMSKY: Well, I'm looking for a new theory too, and I always have been. In fact, I don't see how anybody can ever do anything different. You mention paradigms. I think when Tom Kuhn was discussing paradigms, he had in mind major scientific revolutions. You know, the Galilean revolution or Einstein or something of that sort. But it seems to me to cheapen, to demean the whole concept to apply it to....

RIEBER: Do you mean to say that you do not think that you have not been involved in major scientific revolution in psychology.

CHOMSKY: Well, to compare it to the revolutions in the natural sciences is quite improper. The kind of work I've been associated with has earlier antecedents, and builds very definitely and explicitly on them. There are differences in point of view, but quite honestly I don't think that I've suggested anything in the human sciences beyond what I've been stressing here over and over again, namely, let's apply the canons of rationality that are taken for granted in the natural sciences. And when we do, some things will be fairly obvious. Beyond that, I've tried to discover the properties of a particular cognitive system.

RIEBER: If you haven't really revolutionized the ideas, perhaps you've revolutionized the interests.

CHOMSKY: My own feeling is that anything I've done in the study of language or in other fields is hardly more than the application of normal standards of rationality, which have been taken for granted in the natural sciences for centuries, to phenomena in these fields. When you do, some things are immediately obvious. For example, it's immediately obvious that language involves a discrete infinity of

constructions, that grammar involves iterative rules of several
types. That is where the serious work begins, and I do think that
many quite interesting ideas have been developed and explored in the
past 30 years or so by pursuing these questions, that is, in the work
on generative grammar. But it seems almost transparent that the
general approach is a natural one, although it would have been
difficult to pursue it without the stimulus of the developments in
the theory of formal systems in the past century. I feel the same
way about our discussion of cognitive structures as "mental organs" —
that is, about a modular rather than uniform theory of the mind, and
also about the great significance of innate determinants of mental
growth. Again, all of this seems transparent, as soon as you face
the questions without prejudice. Or take the questions we discussed
concerning "psychological reality." Again, what seems to be a
fundamental error undermining the whole debate over this issue is
clear enough as soon as we drop certain prejudices. In fact, quite
generally, as we're able to peel away certain layers of traditional
dogmatism, it seems to me almost obvious what the general mode of
proceeding ought to be. I wouldn't regard that as a "paradigm
shift." Nor do I think that a lot of the currently fashionable talk
about repeated paradigm shifts makes any sense. It's striking in
the social sciences.... I've read articles by linguists and
psychologists who talk about paradigm shifts that come every two
years or so. In physics they come once in two centuries. This is
just nonsense. Of course, we ought to be looking for new theories
all the time. The existing theories in these domains are hopelessly
inadequate, and therefore we try to improve on them, or construct
them on a new basis. If I were to accept now what I myself had
proposed twenty years ago, I'd quit the field. That would be enough
to show that it's not a worthwhile field to be in.

RIEBER: Twenty years ago you proposed something that had a
fundamental impact on the development of both linguistics and
psychology. You started a movement which, perhaps might have
happened without you, I don't know, but it's hard to believe that
behaviorism was going to go out so rapidly as it did without the
impact that you had on it. I know it's hard to look at yourself in
historical perspective, but it seems to me that you did have a rather
major impact on the shift from a very strongly behavioristically-
oriented profession to a profession that is very much different at
present.

CHOMSKY: I think that behaviorism in any of its variants had
essentially run its course. Its accomplishments have to be absorbed
in the psychology of the future, but the stranglehold on thought that
it imposed had to be broken, and twenty years ago — to take the
moment in time that you mentioned — this was happening from several
points of view. More fundamentally, I feel that it is necessary to
disentangle psychology from its antecedents in empiricist learning
theory and to approach its problems afresh. If you ask what

psychology should be doing, what new theory it should be looking
for, my feeling is — repeating once again — what it ought to be
doing is trying to study the human mind and its growth and its
manifestations much as we study any complex problem in the natural
sciences. We should try to isolate the specific sub-systems that
enter into a very complex interaction in the comprehensive abstract
system that we call the mind, and also to find the physical basis
for these specific systems, if we can. We should be looking for
the principles that govern the structure and functioning of those
systems, as well as their interactions, and we should also try to
unearth and make explicit the innate properties that determine their
growth. That is where the significant theories are going to arise,
I would guess. It may be that someone will come up with a radically
new way of thinking about these questions, but it is not obvious
that one is required, at least with regard to the questions we have
been discussing today. There are many questions that we haven't
discussed at all — for example, questions about the causation of
behavior, the exercise of will, choice, and so on. About these
questions, I have nothing to say and I know of nothing substantive
to repeat that others have put forth. I've tried to make a distinction elsewhere between "problems" and "mysteries" — the former
involving questions that give rise to intelligible and perhaps
promising research programs and the latter lying beyond our cognitive
grasp, perhaps for contingent historical reasons or perhaps for
deeper reasons: we are, after all, biologically given organisms with
our particular intellectual scope and limits, not "universal
creatures," capable of comprehending anything. The fact that we can
construct intelligible scientific theories in some domains presumably
results from intrinsic capacities that may very well limit, in
principle, the scope of our understanding. Such speculations aside,
we have been discussing here what I would like to call "problems",
in this sense, but there are other questions that still, and perhaps
for us forever, fall into the domain of mysteries, questions of the
causation and choice of action among them. But keeping to questions
relating to the structure of cognitive systems and the determinants
of their growth, I think there are quite a lot of open questions and
some reasonable programs of research designed to study them, in quite
a few domains. The particular domain into which I put most of my
energies, the structure of language, seems to me to have been a very
exciting one just in the last seven or eight years. I don't pretend
to speak for any consensus in the field here, in fact, I'm in a very
small minority in the field in this respect, but I believe it's been
possible in the past few years to develop a theory of languages with
a degree of deductive structure that provides a kind of unification
and explanatory power going well beyond anything that would have been
imagined even a decade ago. Again, I don't think many linguists
agree with me about this — but that's the way it looks to me. Let
me stress again, so there is no confusion about it, that with regard
to what I just said, I suppose I'm in a very small minority in the
field today. But then, that has always been the case. With regard

to me, it doesn't seem very different now from what it was ten or
twenty years ago. But my own views are not what they were then,
and I hope they will not be the same ten years from now. Any person
who hopes to be part of an active growing field will take that for
granted.

DIALOGUE II

Charles Osgood's Views on the Psychology of Language and Thought

Charles E. Osgood is Professor of Psychology and Research Professor in Communications at the University of Illinois. He served as Director of the Institute of Communications Research until 1965, when he was appointed as a Professor in the Center for Advanced Study at Illinois. His major areas of concern have been research and theory construction in the psychology of language (psycholinguistics), including cross-cultural research in (now) 30 human societies around the world, and on the psychology of interpersonal, intergroup and international relations, including development of the GRIT strategy (Graduated and Reciprocated Initiatives in Tension-reduction). In the first area of concern, he is author of Method and Theory in Experimental Psychology (1953), a graduate textbook, The Measurement of Meaning (1957) with Suci and Tannenbaum, Cross-cultural Universals of Affective Meaning (1975) with May and Miron, and Lectures on Language Performance (1980); in the second area of concern, he is author of An Alternative to War or Surrender (1962), Perspective in Foreign Policy (1966), and Mankind 2000 ?? (1980, in progress). He has also published numerous articles in both of these areas of concern over the past 40 years. He has served as a consultant to various government agencies — including the Air Force, the Navy, and the Arms Control and Disarmament Agency.

Osgood went to high school in Brookline, Massachusetts, where he became editor of both the weekly newspaper and the monthly short-story magazine. He did his undergraduate work at Dartmouth College and received his B.A. degree in 1939 — as well as an honorary degree of Doctor of Science in 1962. He did his graduate work at Yale University, receiving the Ph.D. degree in 1945. After two years of psychological research with the Air Force (in Salina, Kansas) and the Navy (at the submarine base in New London, Connecticut), he was

appointed as an Assistant Professor in Psychology at the University
of Connecticut. In the fall of 1949 he was invited to the University
of Illinois as an Associate Professor — and has been there ever since.

Professor Osgood is a past president (1963) of the American
Psychological Association, and in 1960 he received this association's
aware for Distinguished Contribution to the Science of Psychology.
In 1971 he received the Kurt Lewin Award for Contribution to the
Solution of Social Issues; in 1972 he was elected to membership in
the National Academy of Sciences and in 1977 was elected an honorary
life member in the New York Academy of Sciences. In 1976 he received
the first award given for cross-cultural research by the Interamerican
Congress of Psychology, and he was named as the Linguistic Society
of America's Professor for its 1978 Summer Institute. He has been a
Fellow with the Social Science Research Council, Guggenheim Fellow
(1955-56; 1972-73), and a Fellow at the Center for Advanced Study in
the Behavioral Sciences (1959-60).

Dialogue II. Charles Osgood's Views on the Psychology of Language and Thought

I. What role does cognition play in the acquisition and the development of language? Do linguistic factors influence general cognitive development?

OSGOOD: The first thing I suggest is changing the order of these two sub-questions. Cognition is involved in both pre-linguistic, perceptual information processing, of course, and this is prior to linguistic processing. When I looked at you just now, you were nodding, and I got a certain meaning from it — that you were agreeing — and there was no language involved in that exchange.

As Watt (1970) put it in the Hayes edited volume, the "deep" mental grammar (MG), must be shared by both linguistic and non-linguistic perceptual channels, in adults as well as children. He also concludes that this MG must be equated with what he calls <u>an abstract performance grammar</u> (APG), and this cannot be characterized by a purely linguistic (competence) grammar (LG). This is where the title of my in-progress <u>magnum opus, Toward an Abstract Performance Grammar</u>, came from — I guess when you get into your mid '60's, you say this! However, an "anticipation" of the <u>magnum opus</u> has recently been published, a small volume titled <u>Lectures on Language Perform-ance</u> (osgood, 1980).

Not only is cognizing via the perceptual (non-linguistic) channel prior in development of the individual — and hence can provide those cognizing structures that will be "natural" in later sentencing — but subsequently there is continuous, intimate inter-action between, and parallel processing in, these channels, utilizing a common "deep" cognitive system which I think is essentially semantic in nature. Similarly, before the species developed language,

69

humanoids obviously had to be aware of the significances of states
and events in their environment, and to be capable of learning to
behave appropriately, if they were to survive — otherwise we just
wouldn't be around today.*

RIEBER: Do you substitute the word "understanding" for
"cognizing" then?

OSGOOD: No, because cognizing involves not only comprehending
the significance of either linguistic messages or non-linguistic
perceptual events, but also expressing, whether it be in sentencing
or in other behaviors. When, walking by a sand-lot baseball field,
you hear a sharp crack, and then your companion shouting "duck!",
the ducking of head is a quite different expression than — when
walking with the same friend on a farm, and he says, "duck" — you
look around to see where that bird is!

RIEBER: So cognizing, then, is understanding and performance
as well.

OSGOOD: A basic, very deep, "mental grammar" as Watt called
it. This is the Representational Level of the cognitive system —
shared interactively by both the non-linguistic channel (perceptual
signs of entities and relations which have meaning) and the
linguistic channel (NPs and VPs which have meaning), with these
channels interacting all the time. So, obviously, as far as
acquisition goes, if cognitive structures are based primarily on
pre-linguistic experience — both in the species and in the developing human individual — perceptual cognizing plays a terrific role,
and, most significantly, such cognizing is universal for humans,
regardless of what language they end up speaking.

I have a little diagram here where the vertical axis is relative
importance and the horizontal axis is age in development: non-
linguistic (perceptual) cognizing plays the entire role for the
first few months, and is dominant even up through the first two or
three years: it then gradually becomes relatively less important in
the development of language, with purely linguistic factors becoming
relatively more important. But, in very early stages, it's entirely
a dependency relation of language development on development of non-
linguistic cognizing, with this development influencing the development of language.

What I call simplex sentencings have structures most obviously
based upon pre-linguistic cognizing: perceptual experiences, involving meaningful entities that are linked cognitively in either stative

*And the way things nuclear and political are going, we may not be
around much longer! (Footnote added in March, 1979).

or action relations (e.g., THE BALL IS ON THE TABLE / THE BALL
ROLLED OFF THE TABLE), set up the most basic cognitive structures.
Since these structures already exist when the child begins simplex
sentencings (both in comprehending and, typically somewhat later, in
expressing), what could be more natural than for the child to utilize
these structures in the language acquisition process? In other
words, as the child's linguistic systems develop, these already-
existing cognitive structures are utilized as much as possible.

This is the basis for what I, therefore, call the Naturalness
Principle: the greater the correspondence of the surface structures
of sentences to the underlying, pre-linguistically determined,
cognitive structures, the earlier such sentences will begin to
appear in development and the more easily they will be processed
by adults. This principle applies to complexes (sentences with
conjoined clauses) as well as to simplexes (single-clause sentences):
thus, since THE BALL HIT THE DOLL (and so then) THE DOLL FELL OVER
AND BROKE is the (necessarily) natural order of events as perceptually
experienced, because the ball struck the doll, it (the doll) fell
over and broke will be more natural (earlier acquired and more easily
processed) than will be the doll fell over and broke because the ball
hit it (the doll).

In a number of recent experimental studies on adult processing
(Osgood and Tanz, 1977; Osgood and Bock, 1977; Osgood and Sridhar,
1979), we have found that sentences which correspond to the natural,
pre-linguistically-determined, structures are, indeed, processed
more easily by adults. In one study with children (Osgood and Zehler,
1979), three-year-olds were found to be limited in both Simply
Describing (expressing) and Simply Acting Out (comprehending) to the
natural ordering of bitransitives (THE DADDY DOLL GIVES THE BALL TO
THE GIRL DOLL): four- and five-year-olds — who could process unnaturally ordered bitransitives (THE DADDY DOLL GIVES THE GIRL DOLL
THE BALL) in prototypical cases — reverted to the natural order when
the materials were either non-prototypical or complex (e.g., double
transfers).

Much earlier I had published a paper on Simply Describing
(Osgood, 1971), titled "Where Do Sentences Come From?", reporting
the sentencings by 26 adults of 32 perceptual demonstrations with
ordinary entities in simplex and complex action and stative relations
(and with CEO as "the man"!). What was remarkable was the rarity of
unnaturally ordered sentencings by these adult subjects (who were
students in my graduate seminar in Psycholinguistics, by the way).
Even when I deliberately manipulated entity salience to produce, e.g.,
passives (A NEW BIG ORANGE BALL IS HIT BY THE FAMILIAR OLD LITTLE
BLACK BALL), the typical sentencings were the black ball rolled and
hit a big orange ball — and only one subject produced only two
center-embedded sentences, despite multiple opportunities (e.g., the
tube the ball is on is on the plate), and this was one of my research
assistants, Sarah Smith!

During the summer of 1975, Drs. Fritz Larsen and Chris Tanz, along with cinematographer Gaylert Burrow and CEO, produced a 70-demonstration color film: our Center for Comparative Psycholinguistics now has the Simply Describings by native speakers of 20 languages in our 30-culture sample. My present research assistant, S. N. Sridhar (a linguist, now rapidly becoming a psycholinguist, too) is analysing the some 42,000 sentences produced, looking particularly for (and finding) evidence on how pre-linguistically-based <u>universal</u> cognitive distinctions are differently, but equivalently, made in the surface structures of these diverse languages.*

II. How is the acquisition and development of language influenced by interpersonal and intrapersonal verbal and nonverbal behavior?

RIEBER: Do linguistic factors influence general cognitive development?

OSGOOD: Yes, this obviously is the case — and, as I've said, this influence increases with age. The extent to which language can influence cognition is evident, for example, in the development of reasoning: although many studies have been done on reasoning in adults (e.g., by Wason and Laird, 1972; by Huttenlocher and Higgins, 1971; and by H. Clark, 1971, 1972), I am not aware of research on actual development of reasoning in children.

RIEBER: With regard to metaphor, abstraction, and thinking in general — how do these factors influence cognitive style?

OSGOOD: I suspect that cognitive style is <u>more</u> influenced by non-linguistic and non-perceptual factors. Motivational salience dynamics — inherent semantic vividness, focus of the speaker, and topicality — may cause the speaker to produce, for example, cleft sentences: coming home after a long hard day, one may delare, "A martini, I will have!" 'Way back in 1953, at the psycholinguistics summer seminar in Bloomington, Indiana, an example occurred which shows how motivation of the speaker can produce what would superficially seem to be an ungrammatical (although certainly acceptable) sentence: at a farewell cookout, Sol Saporta, the first to try the broiled teriyaki, exclaimed "Gárlic, I taste!"

Stylistics is much influenced, I think, by two things: (1) motivation of the speaker (momentary saliences for him, topicality and the like): (2) interpersonal communicative demands upon the speaker in ordinary conversation with others (most obviously,

---

* Analysis and reporting of the data for 10 of these languages constituted Sridhar's doctoral thesis (1980).

questions by others which highlight the when, how, where etc. of
things) — and, of course, these interact. I don't think linguistics,
per se, influences style. If anything, it's just the reverse. The
"style" of one's language is a function of personal interest,
motivation and personality. It influences how he makes use of the
resources available in the language. Often, as I said, producing
perfectly understandable sentencings — such as garlic, I taste!
or on fire, Daddy, your pants! — which may be ungrammatical, but
at the same time are highly communicative and common. Any performance theory must take them into account.

Interestingly, there are big pressures now going on to extend
linguistics into this fuzzier domain. One can see this in the
recent volume, Papers from the Para-session on Functionalism, of the
Chicago Linguistic Society (Grossman, San and Vance (Eds.), 1975);
with relatively little concern about "grammaticality" in the usual
sense, many of these papers are devoted to the functions of language
in ordinary use, getting at non-linguistic determinants of language
behavior, and thus moving toward a performance (as contrasted with
a competence) grammar. Similarly, the whole pragmatics movement:
younger linguists are going beyond the transformational generative
grammar (TGG) we associate with Chomsky and moving toward an abstract
performance grammar (APG), and thus more and more common ground
between psychology and linguistics is opening up — and psycholinguistics is becoming more truly interdisciplinary.

Linguists seem to be moving away from "competence" criteria
and toward "acceptability" criteria. Another volume of Speech Acts
(edited by P. Cole and J. L. Morgan, 1975) further illustrates this
trend. For just one little example: when asked at the dinner table,
"Can you pass the salt?", most people will simply pass over the salt;
just imagine the social impasse if the listener were to say, "Yes,
of course I can", but then just go on eating and not pass the salt!
In other words, "Can you pass the salt?" is not interpreted literally
as an inquiry about competence, but rather pragmatically as a
request. But note the "knowledge of the world" constraints here:
while "Can you play chess?" and "Can you open the safe?" are
ambiguous, "Can you eat highly seasoned food?" and "Can you understand this message?" are unambiguous inquiries about competence.

RIEBER: Why are these "movements" in linguistics occurring?

OSGOOD: Because, in order to satisfy the criterion of
explanatory adequacy, linguists are being forced into areas of human
communication far beyond the TGG competence base. New research and
data by linguists is pushing them away from competence grammar and
toward what I would call a performance grammar. I suspect that in
the next generation of linguists, although there will still be "pure"
linguistics departments, there will also be new interdisciplinary
departments developing — for examples, departments of psycholinguistics, of sociolinguistics, and even of communolinguistics!

RIEBER: You made that prediction in your Dinosaur Caper (Osgood, 1975).

OSGOOD: Yes, but the movement seems to be happening faster than I expected.

RIEBER: Do you think Halliday's work exemplifies this in any way?

OSGOOD: Partially. He was particularly involved with distinctions between the theme-rheme, topic-commentary, given-new sort of thing — very much, as a linguist, in the forefront of those I've mentioned earlier. The whole sociolinguistics movement is progressing this way.

RIEBER: How is the acquisition and development of language influenced by inter- and intra-personal verbal and nonverbal behavior? To return to topic II!

OSGOOD: Let me first say something about intrapersonal and non-verbal behavior. Here, I think that pre-linguistic determination, again, plays a major role. The child already has acquired all of those perception-based cognizing structures I elaborated on before. One can quite reasonably make the assumption that there is an inherent salience in pre-linguistic perceptual cognizing of the (usually +Animate, often +Human) Source of an action relation as compared with the (often -Animate and usually relatively passive) Recipient of the action. Thus active the cat jumped on the pillow is more Natural than passive the pillow was jumped on by the cat. Similarly there is a greater salience for the Figures of stative relations as compared with the Grounds — compare natural the cat is on the pillow with unnatural the pillow is under the cat. This greater inherent semantic salience of Figures over Grounds is one of the major contributions of Gestalt Psychology, as you well know. Now, one could say, of course, the cornfield is around the cow, but it is simply much more Natural to say the cow is in the midst of the cornfield — COW being perceptually the Figure and CORNFIELD the Ground.

Of course, this postulation of "SVO" structure for pre-linguistic cognizing raises some serious theoretical and empirical problems itself. Roughly 40% of human languages are not SVO in basic typology. Although VSO languages (10%) are found mainly in small and isolated groups of humans, SOV languages are spoken by many major societies, mainly (but not exclusively) in Asia. The Naturalness Principle seems to predict (a) that non-SVO languages will be somewhat more difficult to process and (b) that children acquiring them will, in the early stages, display strong SVO tendencies. So we have a basic question: Why are there ANY SOV or VSO languages?

Although it is true that all languages provide speakers with means of transforming basic structures into orderings that better express their momentary communicative intentions — and that elites in cultures may try to distinguish themselves from the hoi polloi by using non-natural structures (which, of course, the hoi polloi eagerly adopt!) — such an explanation seems insufficient. Note, first, that S-before-O is a universal ordering principle for all language types, this fitting the ±Directionality feature above (Figures of states more salient than Grounds; Sources of actions more salient than Recipients). Note, second, that while Entities (S's and O's) are directly perceptible, the stative or action Relations (V's) must be inferred from the stable (stative) or unstable (action) relations among entities.

While dominant SVO-ers have opted for one Naturalness Principle (which locates the inferred Relations in their "relation" place), SOV-ers have opted for another (which highlights the perceptible Entities over the nonperceptible Relations), and the VSO-ers opt for yet another (which highlights the nonperceptible Relations over the perceptible Entities — which may explain their rarity!). In other words, although SVO may correspond most closely to Naturalness in perceptual cognizing, other salience dynamics may also influence ordering in languages.

There is some relevant evidence on all this for language development in children acquiring various languages (and there will undoubtedly be much more by the time this volume is published). Radulović (1975) did her thesis (under Dan Slobin's direction) on sentencing development of Serbo-Croatian-speaking children in Dubrovnik, Yugoslavia: two children were studied longitudinally (hours and hours over the first two years of life, during the crucial two- to three-word transition period) and a sample of other children was tested on a cross-sectional age basis. What she found for the two children studied intensively was that — although their mothers in short sentences addressed to their children used a large variety of word orderings — the children in this crucial two- to three-word sentencing period used very rigid SVO ordering. Although Serbo-Croatian is basically an SVO language, it is also highly inflected — and it is this which allows the flexibility in word ordering. However (interestingly enough!), the children studied by Radulović began varying word order only after the inflectional system has been established in the theoretically basic SVO ordering.

A bit more recently, S. N. Sridhar (a native speaker of Kannada) and Annette Zehler (a fluent speaker of Japanese as a second language) — both graduate students working with me at the time — received grants jointly from the Center for International Comparative Studies (Joseph B. Casagrande, Director) and the University of Illinois Research Board to test the hypothesis — in Bangalore and Hiroshima, respectively — that in both Simply Describing (production) and

Simply Acting Out (comprehending) very young children would be
beginning their sentencings with SVO rather than the SOV orderings
of their adult models. However, the data for both indicated that —
contrary to expectations — the children were already mirroring
dominance of the adult SOV ordering of both two- and three-word
sentences. We suspect that this may have been because only simple
two-entity action cognitions were used in these studies. Why this
hunch? Because, even more recently, when Dr. Farideh Salili
replicated an experiment by Osgood and Zehler on comprehending and
producing more complex three-entity bitransitive cognizing with
Farsi-speaking (also SOV) children in Iran, 90% of the production
in the Simply Describing situation turned out to be SVO orderings —
even up to the age of 5 years!

What I call part 2 of question 2 — how language development
is influenced by interpersonal relations — is beautifully illustrated in the first paper in the issue of the journal you edit I just
got, "Processes and Products of Imitation: Additional Evidence that
Imitation is Progressive." In this paper, what Ernst Moerk (1977)
does — working with kids and babysitters rather than mothers — is
to demonstrate the sentential complexity of children's imitations of
their babysitters at all levels of development. He finds that the
imitative sentences of these kids (imitating the babysitter
semantically and grammatically) are more complex than their own
spontaneous productions at each developmental level.

Notice what this implies (and again we go back to neobehaviorism): just like Hobert Mowrer in his formal research with
parakeets, myna birds, etc. in the 1950s, I found with my own
parakeet informally many years ago that if it has certain little old
phrases like "Hello, Patty" it has already leaned and says all the
time, the bird will not pay attention when you say it. But when you
introduce a new phrase, like "Merry Christmas," "Merry Christmas" —
even if the bird is flying around or perched on the curtain rods
(like the child playing etc.) — when you say this novel thing, the
bird will fly over to your hand, cock its head, and listen (and so
too the child) and soon will add this to its own repertoire.

You have here the interesting business of adults, usually
unintentionally, setting up models for the child. And, for the child,
when he imitates the adult, there is auditory feedback which can be
checked against the model. So when the child spontaneously produces
this more complex form, and it does match the model that it's heard
from the babysitter, then it sounds right — a lovely case of
secondary reinforcement. Something associated with the affectively
positive babysitter (or the mother, etc.) is being selectively,
differentially, reinforced — and what this paper by Ernst Moerk
shows is that, regularly, the imitations are more complex than are
the spontaneous productions at any stage of development.

III. Are the verbal and nonverbal signal systems interrelated?

First, let me again emphasize the intimate parallelism between the perceptual and linguistic channels in cognizing. As you may have noted, the section of my APG "outline" running from pages 14 to 24 is titled — reversing appropriately that of Roger Brown's first book — "Things and Words," * because, as I have stressed, cognizing of "things" is prior to cognizing of "words." And, as I also noted earlier, this priority must have applied to the development of language in the species as well as it does to contemporary human individuals. Second, let me illustrate the intimate parallelism between perceptual and linguistic channels with two basic neo-behavioristic principles.

An "Emic" Principle applies to situations where (a) percepts are variable but their significances are constant (in comprehending) and (b) where intentions are constant but programs for behaving are variable (in expressing). Within the perceptual channel, for example, the percepts of a desired APPLE object will vary with distance of the child from it, yet the "apple" significance will remain constant; behaviorally, while the APPLE-obtaining intention remains constant, the child first approaches, then reaches and grasps, and only then, with crooked elbow, opens the mouth for a bite (for him to make biting, then grasping, then reaching responses — all in thin air! — as he approaches APPLE would be ludicrous). Within the linguistic channel, similarly, the same "Emic" Principle operates: for example, for all synonyms at the wording level and for all paraphrasing at the sentencing level, and the same naturalness in ordering applies (for Caesar to have announced "vici, vidi, veni" would have been just as ludicrous as the child making biting movement in thin air).

An "Ambiguity" Principle applies in situations where (a) percepts are constant but significances are variable (in comprehending) and (b) where intentions are variable but programs for behaving are constant (in expressing). Within the linguistic channel, most words in a language are to some degree polysemous (including homonymy) — e.g., he went to the BANK, it was a LIGHT one; and exactly the same holds within the perceptual channel — not only for familiar ambiguous figures like the Necker Cube, but also for the meanings of the facial expressions of men in a picket line. On the other side of this coin, linguistically "he was a Colt last year but now he's a Bear" as spoken is quite ambiguous (to the non-sportsaholic, at least!), as is "can you play chess?" as being requestive or

---

*At the time of my original editing of this interview (June, 1979), a paper of mine by this title was in press in a book on verbal and nonverbal communication being edited by M. R. Key; at the time of my final editing (December, 1980), this volume had just been published (See Osgood, 1980).

information-seeking; and, again similarly in the perceptual channel, the combination of a tight-lipped smile with a shaking of a fisted hand is ambiguous as to whether the intent is to threaten or to express successful completion of an effortful task — until, if it is a boxer, the viewer knows whether it is just before or just after winning the fight!

Third (and finally), let me give a few of the many examples of this intimate parallelism from everyday life. Imagine how flabbergasted you would be if, while riding up in an elevator, the only other occupant were to suddenly say "Pick it up!" Commands of this sort imply some appropriate perceptual context (a dropped banana-peel, say). Note how utterly ludicrous emphatic gestures are if misplaced — compare natural "I will nót/HAND-BROUGHT-DOWN-SHARPLY wear that ridiculous tie!" with unnatural "I will nót wear that ridiculous tie/SAME GESTURE!" But my favorite example is this: two co-eds, walking along a campus path, see a third girl approaching with a mini-mini-skirt on; after she has passed, one says to the other, "She álso dyes her hair!" Note first that the use of anaphoric she implies a prior cognition (which could only be perception-based) and second that the also identifies this prior perceptual cognition as something like (THAT GAL / IS WEARING / A REALLY SHORT SKIRT).

Of course, gesturing and facial expressions normally accompany ordinary communication via language. There is nothing quite so worrisome as someone whose gestures are entirely inappropriate or who displays an absolute lack of facial-gestural parallelism while communicating — and, in fact, such behavior is one of the surest signs of mental abnormality. The inescapable conclusions would seem to be these: (1) the "deep" cognitive system is semantic in nature, (2) that it is shared by both perceptual and linguistic information-processing channels, and (3) that sentencing in ordinary communication is always context-dependent.

IV. *How can one best deal with the issue of nature versus nurture in our attempts to unravel the basic issues in the field of language and cognition?*

   (a) *Of what importance is the biological basis of language perception and production?*

   (b) *Of what importance is the study of individuals who suffer from pathological conditions of language and thought?*

My first reaction to the general question is that either extreme is obvious nonsense. Chomsky's extreme "nature" position has really never been documented in any convincing way — it is just an expression of "faith" about the innateness and specificity of language to the human species. All of the recent research with

chimps etc. is making it look less and less likely that the cognitive
capacities involved are unique to language or to humans; I have
stressed the role of pre-linguistic perceptual cognizing, and this
is certainly shared by other species. In my opinion, Chomsky's
extreme innate position is completely untenable.

It is perfectly obvious that a child does not develop and mature
to speak a language — a child of Japanese-speaking parents does not
acquire Japanese any easier than any other human language. However,
both the child's innate cognitive capacities and learning via early
pre-linguistic experiences are probably universal in humans,
equipping children to acquire any human-type language. Thus both
Nature and Nurture combine to make it possible for any normal human
child to acquire any human-type language.

At the other extreme we have B. F. Skinner, who proposes to
complete table rasa at birth. There is nothing innate and everything
is acquired via single-stage S-R conditioning.

RIEBER: He does not deny innateness, he simply minimizes it
so as to not have it make any difference.

OSGOOD: I fail to see what distinction you're suggesting, since
Skinner's theorizing is devoid of innateness. It would deny even
the innate determination of figure versus ground, coming from Gestalt
theorizing.

RIEBER: How do you feel about that?

OSGOOD: A simple example: If you have pairs of verticle lines
separated by space — thus || || || || — you tend to see them as
groups. But now note this: if you just add brackets — thus
][ ][ ][ ][— you get an entirely different grouping perception.
Demonstrations of this sort — and there are many of them — rule
out any simple-minded S-R behaviorism.

Many linguists and psycholinguists use behaviorism as a whipping
boy these days — which is not really abnormal in scientific
controversy, of course! But unfortunately (and polemically) they
usually select the most simple and unsophisticated model of the
opposing paradigm — the one most often presented to sophomores in
Introductory Psychology. Only rarely are the more complex versions
of behaviorism (even those of Hull and Tolman in the 1930s to '40s)
or of more recent neo-behaviorism — like those of Mowrer (cf., his
1960 Learning Theory and the Symbolic Processes) or even my own
earlier elaborations (cf., my Method and Theory in Experimental
Psychology, 1953, and "Behavior Theory and the Social Sciences,"
1956) — analysed in any detail and critiqued (Fodor, 1965, and elsewhere is an exception). The usual arguement, sans elaboration, goes
like this: Chomsky demolished Skinner (with reference to his 1959

review of Skinner's 1957 Verbal Behavior) and Fodor reduced Mowrer
and Osgood to single-stage Skinnerianism — Q.E.D.! All of which,
I guess, is testimony to the fact that science can be faddish.*

So much for internecine warfare! Getting back to our main
theme, let me suggest that — before we can even ask the question
of Nature versus Nurture in language development — we must ask ourselves this: "What Is a Language?" I asked myself this question in
a recent paper by this title.** After making an essential distinction between criteria for anything being "a language" and something
being a human language, I came up with some criteria, but I can only
briefly summarize them here.

Defining Characteristics of Language Generally

Using hypothetical Octopians (with bulbous bodies on which
flowing kaleidoscopic color patterns appear to be the "language")
who land in a space vehicle in our backyard as a non-human example,
I suggested the following:

(1) A NON-RANDOM RECURRANCY CRITERION: production of identifiable
different and non-randomly recurrent physical forms in some
communication channel. We noted that when Octopian A was color-
patterning, Octopian B typically stood "silently" grey.

(2) A RECIPROCALITY CRITERION: these forms being producible by the
same organism that receive them. The "language of flowers" is
only a euphemism — we humans can't smell back!

(3) A PRAGMATIC CRITERION: use of these forms resulting in non-
random dependencies between the forms and the behaviors of the
organisms that employ them. This is the criterion that there
is communication going on — and it renders figurative phrases
like "the language of art" and "the language of music."

(4) A SEMANTIC CRITERION: use of these forms following non-random
rules of reference to events in other channels. This means
that forms must function so as to symbolize for the users the
not-necessarily-here and the not-necessarily-now — a criterion
that is met neither by the game of chess nor the "game" of
mathematics.

(5) A SYNTACTIC CRITERION: use of these forms following non-random
rules of combination with other forms in the same channel.

---

* In Lecture III of my Lectures on Language Performance (1980) I
  review this debate in critical detail — and do a bit of demolish-
  ing myself!
**A version of this paper appears as Lecture I in my Lectures on
  Language Performance (1980).

Although human languages accomplish this on a "left-to-right" temporal basis of ordering, our Octopians appeard to "flash" the equivalents of whole paragraphs simultaneously, but with spatial ordering rules for their patterns.

(6) A COMBINATORIAL PRODUCTIVITY CRITERION: the users of the forms being capable of producing indefinitely long and potentially infinite numbers of novel combinations which satisfy (1) to (5) above. Note that all of my statements about the Octopians were entirely novel as wholes, yet you comprehended them. However, only by mastering Octopian to the point where we could reproduce similar visual-display questions were we able to test them on these criteria!

Obviously, all human languages must also satisfy the (1) to (6) criteria for anything being a language — and it is emminently clear that all known human languages do. However, as a test case using (hypothetical) pale, eyeless midgets discovered in extended caverns far below the present floors of the Mammoth Cave — who emit very high-frequency pipings from their rounded mouths and apparently listen with their enormous, rotatable ears — we can see what criteria might be used to determine if these creatures have an identifiably humanoid-type language. The criteria seem to fall rather naturally into a structural versus functional dichotomy.

Structural Characteristics of Human Languages

All known natural human languages appear to have the following structural characteristics:

(7) they involve use of the vocal-auditory channel (which, it might be noted, is relatively "light-weight" energy-wise and is minimally interfering with other activities, like tool-making and hunting):

(8) they are therefore non-directional in transmission but directional in reception (with directional reception being a function of the fact that we have a head between out ears, this inter-aural distance yielding phase differences for sound-waves originating in all directions):

(9) evanescence in time of the forms in the channel (this having the advantage of minimizing "cluttering up" of the channel, but the disadvantage of putting a heavy load on the memory — hence the spontaneous development of writing systems); the above characteristics requiring:

(10) integration over time of the information derived from the physical forms (although there is some simultaneous patterning at the phonetic level, all "higher" levels (morphemic, word, phrase, etc.) require temporal integration); and providing:

(11) <u>prompt feedback to the sender of his own messages</u> (allowing
children to <u>model</u> their productions on adults and adults to
<u>edit</u> their own productions).

Note that these structural criteria would rule out the signing
of deaf-mutes as being a <u>natural</u> human language — but the sign
languages which have developed spontaneously all around the world
do clearly meet all of the criteria for something to be a <u>language</u>
<u>((1)</u> - (6) above). What about our little Cave Midgets? Well, tape-
recordings of their high-frequency pipings left no doubt but that
the non-random recurrency (1), reciprocality (2), pragmatic (3), and
semantic (4) criteria for something to be <u>a language</u> were satisfied
in communications during their mushroom-and-worm cultivating
activities. Testing for syntactic structuring (5) and combinatorial
productivity (6) took a bit of doing. But analysing endless visual
displays of ultrasonic piping patterns, one linguist was able to
demonstrate "noun/verb" selection rules (5); a bit later, another
had a brainstorm (not surprising, after consuming a worm-and-mushroom
pizza) and created a computer-based Cave-Midgetese synthesizer,
firmly establishing (6). But what about the functional requirements?

Functional Characteristics of Human Languages

All known natural human languages also have the following
functional characteristics. And, anticipating a bit, we can report
that our intrepid linguists — armed with their ultrasonic Visual-
pattern Display System and a (by now) much improved Cave-midgetese
Synthesizer — were, after much labor, able to conclude that (with
many variations in emphasis and complexity) "the language of the
Cave Midgets" was, indeed, humanoid — developed by an early branch
of primates that, in their search for bigger and better worms and
mushrooms, happened to end up in caverns deep in the earth!

(12) ARBITRATINESS OF FORM-MEANING RELATIONS: <u>the rules relating</u>
<u>forms in the communication channel to events in other channels</u>
<u>are typically arbitrary rather than iconic</u> (we must say
"typically" because human languages do display both onomatopoeia
and phonetic symbolism).

(13) DISCRETENESS OF FORM-SHIFTS SIGNALING DIFFERENCE IN MEANING:
<u>the changes in form that convey changes in meaning are dis-</u>
<u>cretely rather than continuously variable</u> (such discreteness of
shifts at all levels — phonemic, morphemic, syntactic — have
certainly simplified the descriptive task for linguists!)

(14) THE HIERARCHICAL ORGANIZATION CRITERION: <u>the stream of forms</u>
<u>in the channel is analysable into levels of units-within-units</u>
(complex sentences into clauses, clauses into immediate
constituents, constituents into word forms, and words into
morphemes and thence phonemes).

(15) THE COMPONENTIAL ORGANIZATION CRITERION: larger numbers of
units at each higher level of the hierarchy are exhaustively
analyzable as near-simultaneous combinations of relatively
smaller numbers of units at each next lower level (thus potentially infinite numbers of sentences are analyzable into some
hundreds of thousands of word units, these in turn into some
thousands of morphemes, and these into some 40 or so phonemes).

(16) THE TRANSFERRAL-VIA-LEARNING CRITERION: human languages are
transferred to other members of the species, both generationally
over time and geographically over space, via experience (learning) rather than via inheritance (maturation) (there is no
evidence whatsoever that human off-spring "mature" to speak the
same language as their parents, as I have already emphasized).

Now we can return to the Nature versus Nurture question — and more
fruitfully, I think.

First, what about the defining characteristics of language
generally? Most interestingly, it can be shown that criteria (1) to
(6) can be either innately determined or acquired via learning — and
constrasting "language of the bee" with "language of the human" will
make this clear. The well-known "dance" of the bee (including that
of workers freshly hatched) on the walls of the hive accurately
represents by its angle with respect to the sun the direction of a
nectar supply, by its number of turns per unit time the distance of
the supply, and by its number of abdomen-wags the quality of the
nectar — and the "observing" bees faithfully fly off to the new
supply. Clearly criteria (1) - (4) — non-random recurrency, reciprocality, pragmatic non-random dependencies between forms and behaviors,
and non-random semantic rules of reference — are being satisfied;
as far as (5), the syntactic criterion, is concerned, since three
types of forms (direction-, distance-, and quality- indicating) are
being combined non-randomly, this too is satisfied; and as far as
(6), combinatorial productivity, is concerned, the fact that for any
given bee "speaker" or bee "listener" the particular combinations of
indicators must often be novel, this too is being met. So the
"language of the bee" — although entirely innate ("wired in") — is
not a euphemism! The "language of the human," in complete contrast,
can only satisfy these same criteria via learning, therefore being
acquired — simply because the child acquiring any particular
language must learn to comprehend and produce the forms in order to
meet the pragmatic, semantic, syntactic and combinatorial-product-
ivity criteria.

Second, what about the structural characteristics of human
languages? Almost "by definition," many of these criteria — (7)
use of the auditory-vocal channel, (8) therefore being non-directional in transmission but directional in reception, and (11) obtain-
ing prompt feedback of one's own messages — are innately dependent

upon the nature of the vocal-auditory channel and the human nervous
system. I do not include (9), evanescence of forms in the channel,
because it is simply a physical characteristic of sound-waves. However, the fact that (9) requires (10), integration over time of the
information carried by the forms, does raise the Nature/Nurture
issue: it would seem that both innate structural capacities (e.g.,
reverberatory characteristics of neural impulse patterns) and learning capacities of the human central nervous system (e.g., acquisition
of antecedent-subsequent predictive systems) would be involved.

Third, and certainly most interesting, what about the functional
characteristics of human languages? Characteristic (12), arbitrariness of form-meaning relations (relating forms in the communication
channel to events in other channels), certainly implies complex
learning processes, since these relations must be acquired uniquely
for each language — even though a common capacity for learning is
also implied, of course. Characteristic (13), discreteness of form-
shifts signaling differences in meaning, would seem to imply both
Nature (a human nervous system bias toward discrete, all-or-nothing,
shifts of state at all levels rather than continuously graded ones)
and Nurture (just what cognitive states, essentially semantic in
nature, will come to be associated with what form-units at what
levels within the hierarchy must be uniquely acquired for each
particular human language). Similarly, characteristic (14), the
hierarchical organization of the stream of forms into levels of units-
within-units, would involve both innate (the unicersal hierarchical
organization of human brain functioning for languages) and acquired
(the learning of those particular alternate units within each level
which are unique for each language). Again similarly, both Nature
and Nurture contribute to (15), the universal characteristic of
large numbers of units at each higher level being exhaustively
analyzable into relatively small numbers of units at each next lower
level, and for the same reasons. But, finally, (16), the transfer
of human languages to other members of the species over time and
space being via learning rather than maturation, is obviously Nurture
rather than Nature.

RIEBER: The innately-based functional characteristics universal
to human languages — the discreteness of form shifts at all levels
signaling meaning differences, the hierarchical organization into
levels of units-within-units, the exhaustive analysis of units at
each higher level into the smaller number of units at each next lower
level (no left-over pieces!) — strike me as a most remarkable evolutionary achievement.

OSGOOD: True — but you must keep in mind that other higher non-
human species share many of the underlying cognitive characteristics.
And also — harking back to my hypothetical Octopian creatures from
Arcturus — although the way human brains have evolved to accomplish
these communicative ends is extraordinarily efficient, it is not the

only conceivable way (or even, perhaps, the best way) to achieve communicative effectiveness. It's just that, given the way our nervous systems have developed, it's probably the only way humans could have done it.

Now let me say something about your IV (a) — of what importance is the biological basis of language perception and production? — and, in doing so, again assume my dinosaur role! One of the impacts of Chomsky's emphasis (via Descartes) on the rationality of humans as opposed to non-humans — in itself an "irrational" distinction, I think — has been to lead many linguists and psycholinguists to forget that humans are themselves a kind of animal.

Much of my own research over the years has been concerned with the very basic and primitive — one might even say, Neanderthal! — dynamics of human thinking and talking: demonstration of the universality of three affective features of meaning, Evaluation, Potency and Activity (the Good-Bad, Strong-Weak, and Active-Passive of things), now for 30 language-culture communities around the world (see Osgood, May and Miron, 1975); investigation of congruence/incongruence dynamics (not logic, but psycho-logic!) and affective polarity effects (the Yang and Yin of things, Positiveness versus Negativeness) in the processing of words and sentences (cf., Osgood and Richards, "From Yang and Yin to And or But," 1973; Hoosain, "The Processing of Negation," 1973); and demonstration of such primitive dynamics in interpersonal and, even more particularly and frighteningly, in international relations in this nuclear age (cf., Osgood, 1969, with the ridiculous title, "Conservative Words and Radical Sentences in the Semantics of International Politics," and an as yet unpublished address given at a December, 1978, UN colloquium, titled "Psychosocial Dynamics and the Prospects for Mankind").

In my "What Is a Language?" (Lecture I in Osgood, 1980) I also suggest a number of language universals which — while non-defining — are very significant characteristics of human communicating. Among them are the uses of language to propositionalize ("the moon is made of green cheese"), and to prevaricate ("I was not involved in plánning the Watergate Caper"), but also the following: A LEAST EFFORT PRINCIPLE: across all languages and levels of units, a principle of least effort operates statistically, such that the higher the frequency-of-usage level (a) the shorter the length of forms, (b) the smaller the number of such forms, and (c) the larger the number of different meanings (senses) of the forms used. This, of course, was originally proposed by G. Kingsley Zipf (1949); AN EFFECTIVE POLARITY PRINCIPLE: across all languages and levels of units, it is statistically universal that affectively Positive forms are distinguished from affectively Negative forms (a) by marking of the Negative members of pairs and (b) by priority of the Positive members of pairs in both development (of both languages and individual speakers) and form-sequencing in messages. And for this non-defining universal, Greenberg (1966) provides massive evidence at all levels.

However, most relevant to my present concern is THE POLLYANNA
PRINCIPLE: <u>across all languages and levels of units,</u> it is statistically universal that affectively Positive forms and constructions are
more diversified, more frequently used, and more easily processed
cognitively than affectively negative forms and constructions. The
greater <u>diversity</u> of Positives shows up nicely in our cross-linguistic
semantic differential data on 30 language-culture communities around
the world — in the eight-octant space defined "universally" by
<u>E</u>(valuation), <u>P</u>(otency) and <u>A</u>(ctivity) factors, the + + + octant
(Good, Strong and Active) is much more densely populated with concepts
than the − − − octant (Bad, Weak and Passive).

Perhaps the most striking evidence for the Pollyanna Hypothesis
will be offered in a joint in-preparation paper by Osgood and Hoosain,
to be titled "The Pollyanna Hypothesis: II. It is Easier to 'Simply
Get the Meaning' of Affectively Positive than of Affectively Negative
Words," where parallel data for both American English and Hong Kong
Chinese will be presented. With subjects required to simply say
(appropriately) either "positive" or "negative" to <u>single</u> words drawn
from oppositional pairs (but presented randomly, not in pairs), there
is a highly significant difference, averaging about 50 msec., favoring
Positive members (e.g., ANGEL/DEVIL, WONDERFUL/TERRIBLE, TO REWARD/TO
PUNISH, ABOVE/BELOW, SOMETHING/NOTHING etc. for 67 oppositional
pairs). So, it <u>is</u> easier to "simply get the meanings" of affectively
positive than of affectively negative words!

Let me emphasize again: these "gut" dynamics of human thinking
and talking — affective Polarity effects, Congruence Dynamics
(psychologic), and Pollyannaism — are <u>not</u> "rational" processes, and
they operate (usually beyond awareness) on people in high places as
well as low. The sooner human beings appreciate this fact — stop
kidding themselves that <u>they</u> are, unlike other animals, purely
rational beings <u>a la</u> Descartes and accept the fact that they carry
along a Neanderthal within — the sooner they'll be able to <u>think</u>
and <u>act</u> more rationally (as paradoxical as that may seem!) and improve
their prospects in this nuclear age for reaching and going beyond the
Year 2000. In other words, only by understanding how the Neanderthal
Within operates will people be able to understand and control interpersonal — and particularly international — conflicts. You don't
like this? Well, you are not alone. Despite the evidence for such
dynamics at all levels, I have found that even my academic colleagues
in economics, political science, sociology — to say nothing of
people in government — find such questioning of one's own thinking
extremely threatening.

RIEBER: Let's turn now to IV (b) — of what importance is the
study of human beings who suffer from pathological conditions of
language and thought?

OSGOOD: I'm not at all sure what you include in "pathological" — the kind of thinking I've just been talking about could well be considered pathological, and if displayed by individuals (say, a Sam or an Ivan) we would label them paranoid and put them in an institution! Also many of the phenomena studied in sociolinguistics represent deviation from norms, but I don't think we'd call them "pathological." So, let me assume you are referring to deviations from the norm which, like aphasia, involve structural disorders (e.g., brain damage) and not to functional disorders like paranoia.

Although Murray Miron and I did edit a volume titled Approaches to the Study of Aphasia (Osgood and Miron, 1963) — reporting a 1958 summer conference on aphasia held at the Boston VA Hospital and sponsored by the Committee on Linguistics and Psychology of the Social Science Research Council — I certainly cannot claim any expertise in this area. However, as I recall that conference, although the participants agreed that Roman Jakobson's linguistic contributions to research on aphasia has been highly significant, they did not see how Noam Chomsky's Competence Theory led to any distinctive predictions about patterning in aphasic disorders. However, that was long ago.

RIEBER: What can we learn from the study of aphasics about how the brain is programmed?

OSGOOD: I assume you mean how the brain is "programmed" for language processing. As I see it, the problem here as far as psycholinguistics is concerned is that you have to have a theory to test against the rich array of data (on relations of brain damage locations and kinds to types of language disturbance) that already exists. And, obviously (I think), this must be a performance theory, not an abstract, linguistic competence theory. As you know, I now have my own abstract performance theory fairly well developed (again, see Osgood, 1980) — but I have yet to relate it in any detail to the data of aphasia. At some point along the line, though, this might well be a very profitable venture.

RIEBER: How do you feel about a theory that includes some aspect of preverbal cognitive planning in its relationship to an attention-shift which would then, in effect, precipitate some kind of breakdown in fluency such as found in aphasics and stutterers? Would it be a useful paradigm to study?

OSGOOD: Let me first tell you about one study on severely impaired anomic aphasics by Sylvia Scheinkopf (1970) which testifies to the primitiveness of the affective meaning system. In an earlier study of mine (Osgood, 1960) I had developed a graphic differential with visual opposites substituting for the usual verbal ones (e.g., for E, a WHITE versus a BLACK circle; for P, a THICK versus a THIN block-like object; for A, a STRAIGHT versus a ZIGZAG line) and

applied it successfully in a four-culture study. Scheinkopf, using
a slightly modified set of such visual-pairs (each on a separate,
divided card), found that her anomic aphasics performed very much
like normal controls in pointing appropriately to the affectively
congruent sides when given the verbal concepts — despite their
manifest difficulties in naming and word-finding, or even being able
to verbally describe the graphic pairs.

Returning now to your question, I think we should broaden it
from stuttering to hesitation phenomena more generally — since this
is less an emotional disorder and more a common characteristic of
ordinary conversation. Maclay and Osgood (1959) studied such
phenomena in the "speech" (tape-recorded) of 12 scholarly participants
in another SSRC Conference, this one on Content Analysis. We found
several very interesting things — which have been substantiated by
much research of others. Hesitation pauses are not distributed
randomly, but occur more frequently before the more complexly coded
(and less frequently used) lexical words rather than before function
words. It was also the case that filled pauses (with ahs, ums, etc.
inserted) were more likely before function words (thus often before
selection of whole constituents) while unfilled pauses were more
likely before lexical words (as if, already into a constituent, the
speaker is "debating" his choice of the most informational item);
congruently, False Starts (blocking and returning to correct)
typically involved lexical items, whereas Repeats (more like your
stuttering) typically involved function words antecedent to lexical
choices. The likelihood of a filled pause was mainly dependent upon
duration of a nonspeech interval — as if the struggling speakers
were trying to hold onto the conversational ball! Finally, there
were marked individual differences among speakers in their types and
distributions of hesitation phenomena — sufficient to consider them
aspects of "style."

V.   *Of what importance is the current research in comparative
      psycholinguistics (recent attempts to train chimpanzees and/or
      apes via sign language or any other method)?*

Although there is much interesting data now available for sign
language in the chimpanzee — and it is very relevant to the question
of whether language is necessarily the sole competence of the human
species — I am sorry that so little work has been done with the
highly intelligent dolphin. Here is an animal with one of the largest
brains relatively — a mammal, not a fish, sort of like a very bright
dog that decided to live in the oceans — and capable of incredibly
complicated and intimate interactions with humans, yet it has hardly
been tapped for language-like cognitive capabilities. (I might note,
also, that it is shocking the way sea-food industries fishermen,
particularly those based in Japan and the U.S., are literally
murdering the many dolphins that get caught in their nets).

The research being done with chimpanzees and other primates —
and which could be done with the dolphin — has a tremendous amount
to offer psycholinguistic theory. My "What Is a Language?" paper
(also Lecture I in Osgood, 1980) has a whole section on language in
non-human species — from the clam (nil!), to the bee (yes, but all
innate), to the bird (vocal/auditory channel, but minimal pragmatics
and semantics), to the dog (considerable pragmatics and semantics,
but minimal vocal/auditory channel use), to the chimpanzee — and
the reason chimps can't "talk" (vocal-auditory channel) is simply
that, unlike humans with their left hemispheric dominance over the
medial vocalizing system, chimps have no such dominance and hence
cannot finely control vocalic outputs. This, of course, is why the
Kellogg's Gua and the Hayes' Viki — brought up as infant chimpanzees
in a human home just like any child — failed miserably to develop
any language facility: you can't teach apes to talk "human".

The decision of the Garners (R.A. and B.T., 1969) to bring a
baby chimp up in a human environment, but with constant exposure to
the natural signings of deaf-mutes (ASL), was long overdue, and one
of the most exciting psycholinguistic developments in decades
resulted.* I will concentrate on the Gardners' Washoe rather than
on the Premacks' (1972) Sarah; although extensive (and continuing)
laboratory research with Sarah and others demonstrates the astonish-
ingly complex cognitive capacities of a chimpanzee, it is less
obviously relevant to language per se, hence to psycholinguistics.
So now let's check Washoe's communicative performance against our
criteria for something being "a language" (my criteria (1) - (6)
earlier).

Criterion (1) (non-random recurrency of forms) is obviously met
by the differential use (by age 4) of some 80 gestural signs.
Criterion (2) (reciprocality, both sending and receiving) is obviously
met — first with humans "at the other end" but more recently with
other chimps. Criterion (3) (pragmatics) is satisfied by such
evidence as her making the "toothbrush" sign "in a peremptory fashion
when its appearance at the end of a meal was delayed," by her signing
"open" at the door of a room she was leaving, and so forth ad
infinitum. There is also no question about satisfying criterion (4)
(semantics): her learning to sign "dog", mainly to those in picture
books, but then signing it spontaneously to the sound of an unseen
dog barking outside; her signing "key" not only to keys being
presently used to open locks but also to "not-here" keys needed to

---

*I can't resist adding this footnote: a few years earlier, while I
was on the University of Illinois Research Board, a nearly identical
proposal was made by a group here; after some haggling with and
explaining to the physical science and engineering folks on the
board, we OK'd the proposal — but (sob!) the young couple who were
to bring up the baby chimp backed out.

unlock locks! And there is also no question but that criterion (6)
(combinatorial productivity) is satisfied: the Gardners report that
as soon as Washoe had a vocabulary of a dozen or so signs (including
verbs like "open" and "go," nouns like "key" and "flower," and
pronouns "you" and "me," and adverials like "please," "more" and
"hurry") she spontaneously began combining them in sequences like
"open flower" (open gate to flower garden), "go sweet" (to be taken
to raspberry bush), and "you me out" (you take me outdoors).

But what about criterion (5) (syntax)? This has been the focus
of most questioning of Washoe's "having a language," and in early
critiques both Bronowski and Bellugi (1970), and McNeill (1970),
stress the fact that Washoe's "utterances" display no constraints on
"word" order, her signings seemingly having free ordering (e.g. "up
please" or "please up," "open key" or "key open"). However, in an
equally early commentary, Roger Brown (1970) makes the following very
significant point: that just as in human language development, Washoe
displayed a gradual increase over time in the sign-length of her
"utterances" — two common before three and three common before four
— and Brown asks reasonably, "Why should this be so if the sign
combinations are not constructions?"

Perhaps most significantly, Brown observes that ". . . there is
little or no communication pressure on either children or Washoe to
use the right word order for the meanings they intend" when language
is being used in contexts that are perceptually unambiguous to both
producer and receiver — which is the case in much of early child
language and in just about all of Washoe's signings (and it should
be noted that, although Washoe's companions "corrected" the signings
of particular lexical items, they apparently did not "correct" for
sign orderings, as do most adult companions when young human children
begin actual sentencing).

To put a cap on all this, let me now bring into the picture a
more recent study by the Gardners (1975) on evidence for sentence
constituents in chimpanzee versus child — specifically, responding
appropriately to WH-questions. Given a simple "sentence" or perceptual situation: the Q who you (me, that)? should yield the appropriate
person's name; the Q who smoke (go out, etc)? should yield again the
appropriate name; the Q whose shoes (hat, etc)? again correct person
naming; the Q what that (with pointing), should yield correct object
name; the Q where we go (tickle you, etc), the appropriate locative
expression . . . and so on. The Gardner's experiment on this with
Washoe was when she was about 5 years old (and in her 50th-51st
months with them). Most impressive was the contingency of Washoe's
replies correctly upon the form of Q — at the .00001 level of
significance; her responses contained the appropriate sentence
constituents 84% of the time, this being ". . . far beyond anything
that could be extrapolated from the children's data for Stage III" —
here referring to studies by both Roger Brown and Susan Ervin-Tripp.

So much for any argument about there being a sharp line between the cognitive capacities of "rational" humans and those of other higher primates!

VI. What are the most important and promising applications of research in the psychology of language and cognition?

I'm sure that this question will bring forth the personal research interests, concerns and gripes of all your interviewees! I am particularly concerned with what I have already referred to as faddism — not only in linguistics and in cognitive psychology, and therefore doubly in psycholinguistics, but in the scientific enterprise generally. I think it affects editors of journals, selection of members of their consulting boards, reviewers of books — and, therefore of course, the direction of research endeavors by individuals, particularly those younger folks who are (understandably!) upward mobile.

This shows up in the topics of research which are deemed most significant — over the past few years, for example, the topic of memory in cognitive psychology, particularly memory in language behavior; it shows up in the methodology of research — witness the swings in the past decade away from either elaborate statistical methods (e.g., factor analytic techiques) or tight experimental designs in psycholinguistic research toward much looser and more "casual" observational studies of a few or (often) even a single child in language development; and it even shows up in the more subtle attitudes toward the underlying theoretical assumptions behind the research people do — during the '30's up through the '50's anything submitted to journals that had the slightest tang of "mentalism" had two strikes against it, but during the '60's on up to the present '80's (given particularly the impact of Chomsky) anything that has the slightest tang of "behaviorism" has had two strikes against it.

Now, there is nothing inherently wrong about the development and thrust of new topics, methods and theoretical frameworks — just the reverse, they should be encouraged. What is wrong, I think, is the faddish aspect of it. Given the fact that scholars and scientists are also humans liable to the psycho-dynamics I discussed earlier, there are strong, largely unrecognized, pressures to (a) run the fad of the moment into the (non-productive and quibbly) ground and (b) to deny a fair "hearing" to either perfectly good research and theory generated out of older "wrong-tang" positions or even to fresh, creative research methods and theories that do not happen to fit the existing fad. I think such faddism must inevitably have a stultifying effect on the development of any scientific field — and editors, consultants, reviewers, right on down to individual researchers, ought to be less defensive about their own fad of the scientific moment and more on the look-out for new ideas, regardless of their origins. Thus spake the old Dinosaur!

Returning to the actual wording of your question VI, I don't
see how — all of us being human and surely doing what we are doing
in psycholinguistics because we sincerely believe it is ". . . most
important and promising" — one can answer it without either empha-
sizing his own research interests and theoretical biases or lapsing
into rather vague generalities. Sure — I think that research on
language development in children (particularly in relation to pre-
linguistic cognitive capacities) is very important, but so is research
on adult language processing (particularly in the production and
comprehension of complex and unnaturally ordered sentences). I'll
confess that I have some doubts about the relevance for psycholinguistic theory of the rather wild fad of the day generally referred
to as Artificial Intelligence. Why? Simply because humans inevitably
are limited to programming computers in terms of how they think they
themselves process language — and the faithful performance of the
computer tells us literally nothing about how the human brain itself
operates in psycholinguistic performances. But here, too, I am undoubtedly victim of my own biases!

VII. *Do you feel that the field of language and cognition is, as
some believe, in a state of transition searching for a new
theory or paradigm? If so, what kind of theory do you believe
will emerge or is at present emerging?*

Of course I feel that ". . . the field of language and cognition
is . . . in a state of transition searching for a new theory or
paradigm" and that the " . . . kind of theory (that) will emerge (and)
is at present emerging" will turn out to be very much like my Abstract
Performance Grammar (APG)! I'll bet that most of your interviewees
will egoisticly (but understandably) see their own work as pointing
toward the future. I do believe that the impact of the Chomskyan
Abstract Competence Grammar has just about run its course. I am not
saying, by the way, that this impact was not a healthy and fruitful
one — it certainly was — but I think that many linguists, along
with most psycholinguists, are now beginning to look for theoretical
models that move closer to actual language performance in real life
communication situations. However, these must be models that also
take into account the structural and functional regularities revealed
by Chomskyan TGG.

Since this is precisely the thrust that my own developing APG
has been taking, I feel that the only "answer" to this question I
can give is a very brief overview of my in-progress Toward an Abstract
Performance Grammar, with the "Toward" expressing my awareness that
it can only be a hopeful beginning. The most efficient way I can do
this is to give you the essense of the eight lectures in my recently
published Lectures on Language Performance (Osgood, 1980), since this
was intended as an "anticipation" of the full APG volume — anticipatory in part because it doesn't pretend to cover in any detail the
burgeoning literature in psycholinguistics and related fields that
has been building up in the past couple of decades.

Lecture I. What Is a Language?

This chapter offers a set of defining characteristics, both for anything being "a language" and for the structural and functional properties of humanoid languages, along with a number on non-defining but universal characteristics; it also tackles the hoary question of how human languages may have originated.

Lecture II. Things and Words

A capsule life history of behaviorism, from single-stage (Skinnerian) through two-stage mediational (Hullian) conceptions, leads into my own more complex three-level/componential model. On both input (comprehension) and output (expression) sides of the behavioral equation, we have (most peripheral) sensory and motor projection systems, more central sensory and motor integration systems (meaningless percepts for comprehending and Lashley-like programs for expressing), and (most central) the representational mediation (meaningful) system (significances of signs as input and intentions for behaving as output) — these mediational processes being complexly componential in nature (thus behavioral analogues of bipolar semantic features). The remainder of this chapter deals with the "intimate parallelism" of linguistic and non-linguistic (perceptual) cognizing. Considerable use of these notions was made earlier in this interview, as you'll recall.

Lecture III. Paradigm Clash in Psycholinguistics -- Revolution or Pendula Swings?

This chapter also contributed to earlier parts of this interview. It is a gentle blend of very serious critique of the Chomskyan impact and excerpts from my "Dinosaur Caper" address (=975) at an NYAS Conference on Psycholinguistics. Using a frankly marital theme, I trace the development of psycholinguistics: through engagement, particularly the lively activities of the SSRC Committee on Linguistics and Psychology through the 1950's; marriage, consumated in the early 1960 joint papers of Chomsky and Miller and Miller and Chomsky (both 1963) — which might better have been called an elopement, or even abduction, since it was such a one-sided affair; and divorce (as far as I was concerned), foreshadowed by the mutterings of a scientific revolution in the air and the direct paradigm conflict highlighted at a 1966 conference on Verbal Behavior and General Behavior Theory at the University of Kentucky. I discuss the natures of scientific revolutions versus pendula swings — concluding that Chomskyan TGG constituted a genuine revolution for linguistics but clearly not for cognitive psychology (including psycholinguistics) — and suggest some of the lines along which reconciliation seems to be taking place.

Lecture IV. Structure and Meaning in Cognizing

What I call the Little Black Egg (certainly more biological than a Little Black Box!) characterizes the language-cognizing system as being organized in terms of two basic processes — Encoding (transforming perceptual and linguistic input information into sets of semantic feature code-strips, i.e., meanings) and Decoding (transforming the structured semantic cognitions into output behaviors, including utterances) — and in terms of three levels — the most peripheral Projection Level (input icons and output motons), the more central Integration Level (input percepts and output programs, for cognizing and behaving appropriately, linguistically and otherwise), and the most central Representational Level (significances of inputs and intentions of outputs). It is the Representational Level that is at the core of my Abstract Performance Grammar.

The Structural Notions (S-I to S-XI) of my APG involve postulation of four processing mechanisms: A LEXICON transduces meaningless (in themselves) sensory percepts of perceptual and linguistic signs into meaning-full semantic feature code-strips as significances in comprehending and transduces meaning-full intentions into meaningless (in themselves) programs for behaving in expressing, all on a "word-like" basis (cf., Osgood and Hoosain, 1974). An OPERATOR assigns the code-strips received "upward" from LEX to its postulated three components, $(M_1 - - (M) - \rightarrow M_2)$ — i.e., in language, SNP/VP/ONP — on the basis of language-specific constituent boundary cues in comprehending and transmits such sets "downward" to LEX for expression after processing. A BUFFER receives unnaturally-ordered constituents from OPR during processing, holding them briefly, and returning them to OPR after shifts have been made. And a long-term MEMORY receives the whole-constituent code-strips for processed cognitions and stores them vertically from maximum Positiveness to maximum Negativeness in feature codings of M_1's and horizontally in its $M_1, - (M) \rightarrow M_2$ "bins." It should be noted that all processing in the Representational Level beyond LEX is entirely in terms of operations on sets of semantic features — implying that in this APG syntactic distinctions must be represented in semantic terms.

Turning to the "meaning" side of this chapter, three basis functional notions are postulated: F I, a global sign-learning paradigm (essentially, that when percepts that elicit no predictable behavior pattern are repeatedly paired with other percepts which do (e.g., SIGHT OF COOKIE paired with EATING COOKIE), the former will become signs of the latter); F II, a finer feature-learning paradigm (essentially, that differences in percepts associated with reciprocally antagonistic differences in behavior will lead to bipolar semantic features in the LEXICON); and F III, a frequency/recency principle (essentially, that (a) the greater the frequency of elicitation of mediator components (r_{m_i}) in LEX, the shorter will be

their latencies, (b) the more recent the elicitation, the more
available such components, and (c) that massed repetition results
in reduced availability — the semantic satiation effect).

Lecture V. Naturalness in Cognizing and Sentencing

This is the focal chapter of the book. Starting with the
axiomatic notion — that the basic cognitive structures which interpret and initiate sentences are established in pre-linguistic
experience — we arrive at the empirically testable hypothesis that
the more sentences correspond in their surface forms to these pre-
linguistically-based structures, the earlier they will be understood
and produced by children and the more easily they will be processed
by adults.

The Naturalness Notion for simplex sentences (or clauses) is
F IV: postulation of three, primitive, perception-based distinctions
— Substantivity (distinguishing $^+$Substantive Entities from $^-$Substan-
tive Relations), Directionality (distinguishing $^+$Salient Figures and
Sources from $^-$Salient Grounds and Recipients) and Stativity (distinguishing $^+$Stative Relations from $^-$Stative (Action) Relations —
and this leads to a semantic characterization of the most basic
syntax (SNP/V/ONP) of simplex sentences.

F V deals with Naturalness of word-ordering within the constituents of simplex sentences, in both comprehending and expressing, and
specifies the LEX → OPR (in comprehending) and OPR → LEX (in
expressing) interactions involved. It is emphasized (with illus-
trations) that the cures for constituent boundaries are usually
unambiguous and language-specific and also that awareness of such
cues has its developmental origins in comprehending.

Finally, F VI deals with Naturalness in the ordering of clauses
within conjoined complex sentences: natural ordering is that which
corresponds to the order in which events referred to are typically
cognized in pre-linguistic experience (thus after Gramma stuffed the
turkey she roasted it would be natural order, whereas before Gramma
róasted the turkey she stuffed it would be unnatural order). In a
recent paper titled "Unambiguous Signaling of Naturalness in Clause
Ordering: A Language Universal?" Osgood and Sridhar (1979) offers
evidence for English and Kannada, along with 5 other languages in
less detail, that the combined cues of nature plus locus of adverbials
provides such unambiguous cues (e.g., contrast the above after versus
before with the "mindbogglingness" of after or before centered!)
This chapter concludes with a section on Naturalness in Memory
Functioning.

Lecture VI. Pollyanna and Congruence Dynamics — From Yang and Yin
to AND or BUT

       This chapter deviates from the main theme of my APG to bring
into the picture certain primitive and universal affective and
congruence dynamics operating in language behavior — significant
determinants of language behavior that, given the rationalist bias,
have hardly been touched recently by most linguists and even psycholinguists. I begin near the beginning, with the ancient Chinese
metaphysics of Yang and Yin. Then I show how, in linguistics,
Pollyannaism shows up, in the marking (overt or convert) of the
negative members of pairs at all levels, and Psycho-logic shows up
in the congruence rules governing the use of positives and negatives
(see Klima, "Negation in English," 1964, for much evidence). In
psychology, Heider's (1958) balance/imbalance theory, Festinger's
(1957) consonance/dissonance theory, and my own (Osgood, 1960)
congruity/incongruity theory are explicitly concerned with these
dynamics.

       The first major section goes into detail on Pollyannaism —
three ways of being negative (Hoosain, 1973), evidence for the greater
frequency and productivity of affectively positive forms (DiVesta,
1966; Boucher and Osgood, 1969; a new book by Matlin and Stang, 1978),
and a detailing of the recent experiments by Osgood and Hoosain (1980,
in preparation) with English and Chinese reported earlier.

       The second major section details the theoretical and experimental
work we have done on Psycho-logic — presenting a "Mini-theory of
Cognitive Psycho-logic" which leads into the linguistic analysis of
Robin Lakoff (1971) and our own initial experiment with American
English (Osgood and Richards, 1973). This basic design was extended
cross-linguistically to 12 language-culture communities by our Center
for Comparative Psycholinguistics, and a recently published paper of
mine (1979c), titled "From Yang and Ying to And or But in Cross-
cultural Perspective," demonstrates the really remarkable consistency
and significance of the various predictions made about the insertion
of the translation-equivalent ands versus buts in 200 simple sentences
of the type X is ADJ_1 ADJ_2 for each community. This lecture ends
with a sort of coda —— on the finer dynamics of semantic congruence/
incongruence both within and between the constituents of sentences,
involved in polysemy, simile and metaphor (cf., Osgood, 1980, "The
Cognitive Dynamics of Synesthesia and Metaphor").

Lecture VII. Salience Dynamics and Unnaturalness in Sentence
Production

       Here my APG moves fully into a domain of central concern to
linguists (as well as to psycholinguists — or should be!) — the
production and comprehension of unnaturally ordered sentences (transformations, in TGG terms). Here we must first distinguish between

"natural" salience (that with which F IV through F VI in Lecture V were concerned) and "unnatural" salience (with which F VII and F VIII in this and the last lecture are concerned). "Unnatural" salience is that imposed by Speakers upon the (necessarily) natural ordering of the cognitions they start from in order to express their momentary motivation states (perhaps interestingly, I miss in the linguistics literature any concern about why speakers ever produce sentencings other than those generated directly from the deep structures). Needless to say, such shenanigans by Speakers put pressures on Listeners if they are to comprehend!

The first major section here details three major salience variables affecting Speakers: vividness (intrinsic to the intensity of semantic feature codings — e.g., a vámpire and maid dusting the hallway saw); Motivation-of-speaker (a type of salience extrinsic to the normal semantics of constituents, that is attributed by the speaker as a result of his focus (personal interest, involvement, etc.) — leading a concerned speaker, for example, along the path to passivization (e.g., the kéy was taken by somebody, rather than the natural somebody took the key); topicality (another extrinsic type of salience, due to the relatively greater availability (see F III) of the feature-sets representing constituents recently cognized — thus, just having seen my Pierre poodle rush to the window growling at a big black-and-brown dog on "his" lawn, I am more likely in commenting to a house guest to produce that ugly mutt belongs to the Smiths down the street than to produce the Smiths down the street own that ugly mutt).

Kay Bock's thesis made predictions about retaining versus shifting structures in recall with a variety — Dative, Genitive, Passive, etc. — of sentence types (see Osgood and Bock, 1977). What Cooper and Ross in their "Word Order" paper (1975) refer to as the "Me First" principle — spatial deixis, we hunted here and there/* . . . there and here; temporal deixis, I think of him now and then/* . . . then and now; and even WASPness, they played cowboys and Indians/* . . . Indians and cowboys — which also nicely illustrate the dynamics of salience for Ego.

Strictly speaking, F VII — concerned with detection of unnatural orderings within and between constituents by the OPERATOR — applies to Listener comprehension and not Speaker production. However, since (as will be seen) F VIII (I), unnaturalness in sentence production by Speakers, and F VIII (II), comprehension of unnaturally ordered sentences by Listeners, are "mirror images" of each other, I gave these functional notions this ordering. In any case, F VII states in essence (A) that OPR scans semantic features in the order of their behavioral criticality — e.g., primitive (survival-value) affective features prior to denotative features; (B) that OPR checks the constituent code-strips of simplex sentences for Naturalness within and Compatability between on the basic Substantivity,

Directionality and Stativity "syntactic-semantic" features (see F IV);
and (C) that, in comprehending <u>complex</u> (multi-clause) <u>sentences</u>,
similar checks are made on subsequent clauses as the <u>information</u> is
received from LEX. In both (B) and (C), if OPR detects Unnaturalness,
it initiates interactions with the BUFFER designed to restore
Naturalness — as later detailed in F VIII (II).

F VIII (I) is a complex statement and only the essence of it can
be given here. (A) Since in his own behavior as a Listener, the
Speaker-to-be must always naturalize perceptual and linguistic
cognizings in order to comprehend and store them in MEMORY, this
means that he <u>must always start</u> his production process with naturally
<u>ordered cognitions in his OPERATOR</u> — and, if no salience dynamics
are involved, his expressions will have this natural ordering, both
within and between constituents.

Assuming salience dynamics <u>do</u> operate, (B) if the displacement
of constituents (or parts there<u>of</u>), produced by overt expression of
salient non-initial material, leaves the remaining constituents <u>in</u>
<u>natural order</u>, the remainder of the cognition is simply expressed and
no BUFfing is required (EX: if, starting from natural <u>I will have a</u>
<u>martini</u>, salience produces initial expression of <u>a mártini</u>, the
remaining <u>I will have</u> is simply expressed); but <u>(C)</u>, if the displacement leaves the remainder <u>in an order unnatural for expression</u>, the
salient non-initial material is expressed, unnaturally coded remaining
constituent(s) are BUFfed, information remaining in OPR (if any) is
expressed, and then the code-strips from BUF are expressed as they
are returned to OPR (EX: if, starting from natural <u>everyone admires</u>
<u>Napoleon</u>, salient <u>Napóleon</u> is expressed, this leaves <u>everyone admires</u>
(which would be unnaturally ordered if expressed); so the most "leftward" <u>everyone</u> must be BUFfed, remaining <u>admires</u> moves to initial
position and is expressed (but as the passive <u>is admired by</u>, which
has identical semantic coding, except for ¯Directionality), and then
<u>everyone</u> is expressed as returned from BUF).

These two examples of transformation — topicalization (or
"clefting") and passivization — must suffice here. However, similar
types of analyses of a wide variety of transforms of increasing
complexity — for both <u>simplexes</u> and <u>complexes</u> are offered. What is
important about the APG analyses made <u>is this: a relatively small</u>
<u>number of rules governing the nature of salience dynamics and the</u>
<u>OPR/BUF interactions which "compensate" for these dynamics serve to</u>
<u>account for a relatively large and diverse number of transformations</u>
<u>familiar to linguists</u>. Lecture VII concludes a brief section of
literature relevant to salience dynamics and sentence production.

<u>Lecture VIII. Processing of Unnaturally Ordered Sentences in</u>
<u>Comprehending</u>

Salience-motivated unnatural sentencings by Speakers put
Listeners under pressure if they are to comprehend — and <u>they</u> can't

lighten their load by expressing certain information before "natural-izing" the whole. To facilitate production/comprehension processing comparisons, the same transformation-types — in the same general ordering and with many of the same sentential examples — are used here as in Lecture VII; therefore, processing difficulties can be directly compared by literally counting the number of OPR/BUF transfers involved.

Very briefly (necessarily), Section (A) of F VIII (II) indicates, in (1) and (2), that only when Speaker disordering has occurred is Listener re-ordering required — and in (3) that there is no guarantee that our Listener will be successful! Section (B) indicates in (1) and (2) that, when the Listener's OPR has detected cues for dis-ordering of simplexes, if a single cycle of OPR/BUF interactions still leaves an unnaturally ordered cognition, a second cycle is initiated (we were unable to come up with any transformation requiring a triple OPR/BUF cycle) — and, most significantly in (3), that in the processing of complexes, any disordering of either of the simplex clauses must be "naturalized" before continuing processing of the complex. As in F VIII (I) for Expressing, Section (C) here details the interactions involved for Comprehending when use of the BUFFER is required for processing simplexes, and Section (D), similarly, for when BUF is required for processing complexes.

Now let's compare the APG analyses of producing and comprehending of the relatively simple Topicalization example used earlier:

PRODUCTION

Topicalization: I will have a martíni $\Rightarrow$ A martíni I will have

(1) Given SPKR MOT, EXP A martíni $\rightarrow$ (I / will have / ϕ)

(2) EXP remainder, I will have

COMPREHENSION

Topicalization: A martini I (= SPKR) will have $\Rightarrow$ SPKR will have a martini

(1) Since I is unnatural for - - (M) - - $\rightarrow$ slot, BUF a martini $\longrightarrow$ a martini in BUF

(2) Shift remaining constituents "leftward" $\longrightarrow$ (SPKR / will have / ϕ)

(3) Returning a martini from BUF to empty M_2 slot $\longrightarrow$ (SPKR / will have / a martini)

Note that, although the same number of steps (3) are involved in
this case, comprehension requires BUFfing but production does not.

So let us now take a small sample of six transformations —
three simplex and three complex — for which we have APG processing
analyses of the same sentences for both Speaker production and
Listener comprehension. We will use the number of OPR/BUF interactions as an index of predicted processing difficulty. Since each
two-way transfer plus the holding-while-fading in BUF (which must
increase with the N of constituents stacked) is the primary (in
theory) reason for increments in processing time, this would seem to
be the most direct index. N is Natural order, UN is Unnatural order,
and the ( )'s give the number of OPR/BUF transfers.

SIMPLEXES	PRODUCTION	COMPREHENSION
(1) Subject-verb(aux) Inversion:	N ——— (0) ——→ UN	—— (3) ———→ N
(2) Negative AV Preposing:	N ——— (1) ——→ UN	—— (3) ———→ N
(3) Particle Movement:	N ——— (1) ——→ UN	—— (1) ———→ N

COMPLEXES		
(4) Simple Sequence Adverbial:	N ——— (3) ——→ UN	—— (3) ———→ N
(5) Relativized SNP:	N ——— (3) ——→ UN	—— (0) ———→ N
(6) Alter (by Ego) Commentative:	N ——— (3) ——→ UN	—— (5) ———→ N

Only a few of the sentential examples analysed must suffice.
Simplex type (2), I have never been to the White House (N) / néver
have I been to the White House (UN), yields a large difference in
processing difficulty (one OPR/BUF versus three, and five versus
eight steps), in part because, two cycles must be made. In contrast,
Simplex type (3), John looked up the topless waitress (N) / John
looked the topless waitress up (UN), involves only one OPR/BUF
transfer for both — in production, of up while the topless waitress
is moved forward, and, in comprehension, of the waitress constituent
while up is moved forward to fuse with the VP constituent.

For the processing of complexes, note that for all three types
(4 - 6) production involves a constant three OPR/BUF transfers —
always of the non-salient clause$_1$ so that the salient clause$_2$ can be
expressed earlier — thus for type (4), Mary sharpened her hunting
knife (and then) Mary skinned the suckling pig (N) ——→ before Mary

skinned the súckling píg she charpened her hunting knife, and similarly for types (5) and (6). Comprehension difficulty for these
three types varies markedly, however: type (6), for example, going
from Unnatural Mary was annóyed to find John in the bar to Natural
Mary found in the bar John (and) that (= Cog_1) annoyed Mary, involves
BUFfubf naturally Cog_2 (Cog_1 annoyed Mary) and then "naturalizing"
remaining Mary found ──── John in the bar into (strange in English
stylistics, but theoretically natural) Mary / found in the bar / John
(as is easily testable by using the passive transformation) — which
adds up to 5 OPR/BUF interactions!

The second major section of Lecture VIII, first, sets up a
hierarchy of levels of predicted processing difficulty for the entire
gamut of natural and unnatural (transform) types, and second, proposes
a program of systematic experimental research to test the effectiveness of APG predictions of processing difficulty. The predictions
here are based not only on the number of OPR/BUF interactions, but
also on the number of constituents being simultaneously held (while
decaying) and the number of cycles of OPR/BUF transactions — Δ PT
(increment in processing time) being a cumulative function of these
factors.

The experimental research program is limited to comprehension —
the timed judgmental task of the subject being to decide whether each
tape-presented sentence is acceptable ("yes") or anomalous ("no") —
there thus being at each level of predicted difficulty and type of
transform three sentences (separated in time, of course). At the
simplest level, for the Topicality (Clefting) type, a set of these
sentences might by I will have a martini (Natural), a martini I will
have (Unnatural transform), and a mártini I will HEAR (Anomalous).
At a much higher level we might have Causal Sequence, a possible set
of sentences being because the parrot only spoke Portugese, Sailor
Jim sold it to a linguist (N), Sailor Jim sold a línguist the parrot,
because only Pórtugese it spoke (UN), and Sailor Jim sold a línguist
the parrot, because only Pórtugese it ATE (A).

The predicted hierarchy of processing times runs from a minimum
of (0), naturally ordered action or stative simplexes, up to a
maximum of (20), unnaturally ordered, multiply commentative conjoined
complexes (e.g., I regrét télling you that you are fíred) — simply
because this latter was the most complex sentence for comprehending
we analysed. In between these minima and maxima (to give just a
sample), we would have: (1) unnaturally ordered, single cycle
simplexes (like John gave the topless wáitress a sweater); (3) naturally ordered complexes (like Puss scratched Fido and so then Fido
chased Puss); (6) unnaturally ordered, double cycle simplexes with
a single OPR/BUF transfer in Cycle 2 (like néver have I been to the
White House); (18) unnaturally ordered complexes conjoined with
adverbials and with both simplex clauses unnaturally ordered (like
the súckling píg was skinned by Mary after her hunting knife she

sharpened). Note that simplexes and complexes intermingle in the
predicted processing-difficulty hierarchy.

The final section of this final Lecture VIII relates these APG
analyses of natural and unnatural sentence production and comprehension to some of the most relevant literature in the field: (1)
Center-embedding: the Greatest Cognizing Complexity? Beginning with
George Miller's particularly complex example — the race that the
car that the people whom the obviously not very well dressed man
called sold won was held last summer (complete with structural
diagram!) — leads to the APG notions (a) that embedded clauses
always must be prior in cognizing (even if held up in production) to
those that embed them; (b) that, using much simpler single-embedding
examples, the APG rules do in fact handle these phenomena; and (c)
that the double function of NPs (ONP to SNP) can also be handled
within the present rules. (2) Yngve's "Depth Hypothesis" and the
OPERATOR/BUFFER Interactions in this APG. The analysis here leads to
the conclusions (a) that, although similar in purpose, the "Depth
Hypothesis" generates very different predictions about processing
difficulty — and, in many cases, differences which clearly do not
fit ordinary intuitions about processing complexity. Finally, (3)
Some Relevant Linguistic and Psycholinguistic Evidence, provides a
"wrap-up" of this most lengthy and complicated Lecture!

DIALOGUE III

Jean Piaget's Views on the Psychology of Language and Thought

Jean Piaget was born in Neuchâtel on the 9th of August 1896. In 1918 he took his Ph.D. in Natural Sciences at the University of Neuchâtel (Switzerland). Between 1921 and 1925 he was Chief of Laboratory at the Institute Jean Jacques Rousseau in Geneva. Between 1925 and 1929 he was Professor of Psychology, Sociology and Philosophy of Sciences at the University of Neuchâtel. Between 1929 and 1939 he was Extraordinary Professor of History of Scientific Thought at the Faculty of Sciences of the University of Geneva. Between 1929 and 1968 he was Director of the Institute of the Sciences of Education at the University of Geneva. Between 1939 and 1952 he was Professor of Psychology and Sociology at the University of Lausanne (Switzerland). Between 1939 and 1971 he was Professor of Experimental Psychology at the Faculty of Sciences of the University of Geneva. Between 1952 and 1963 he was Professor of Psychology at the Sorbonne (Paris, France). Up to his death in 1980, he was Director of the International Center for Genetic Epistemology at the Faculty of Sciences of the University of Geneva.

He belonged to many Academies and Scientific Societies and was the bearer of more than 35 Doctora Honoris Causa around the world.

His research included primarily genetic epistemology, developmental and experimental psychology in the area of cognition.

His works included: The Origins of Intelligence, The Norton Library, New York, 1952. Judgment and Reasoning of the Child, Littlefield, Adams, Totowa, New Jersey, 1966. Play, Dreams and Imitation in Childhood, The Norton Library, New York, 1962. (With Bärbel Inhelder) The Growth of Logical Thinking from Childhood to Adolescence, Basic Books, New York, 1958. Genetic Epistemology,

Columbia University Press, New York, London, 1970. Structuralism,
Basic Books, New York, 1970. (And alii) Mental Imagery in the Child,
Basic Books, New York, 1971. (And alii) Memory and Intelligence,
Basic Books, New York, 1973. Behavior and Evolution, Pantheon Books,
New York, 1978.

Before his death he focused his interest with the problem of the
epistemology of meaning and reason conducting research in this area.
Among many other prizes he received the Balzan Prize in 1980.

Dialogue III. Jean Piaget's Views on the Psychology of Language and Thought

INTRODUCTION

This chapter is in some ways, different in structure from others. To begin with, it is written in two parts. The first is a presentation by Piaget of his central theme. The second consists of an elaboration of this theme, in response to questions which was developed in collaboration, Piaget treats the problem of the relationships between language and thought from a central point of view, specifically the role of empirical experiments in the context of the relationship between psychology and linguistics.

Furthermore, Piaget handles the question of the role of cognition in the acquisition and the development of language and the influence of linguistic factors on the general cognitive development, from essentially, an epistemological point of view. What follows is his extensive replay to the first two questions that he considered as essential and dominant in the issue between language and thought.

The other questions were partially treated by Piaget who gave this collaborator the main lines of his answers which he left to this collaborator to develop. This plan was followed, as the reader will discover it, for all the other questions and thus reflects Piaget's thinking as well as the written development that this collaborator proceeded to give to Piaget's answers and points of views.

I. *What role does cognition play in the acquisition and the development of language? Do linguistic factors influence general cognitive development?*

In answering this question we shall carefully distinguish between two points: (a) the role of experimentation and (b) the psychological

epistemology that is inherent in empirical experimentation. Experimentation, in a large sense, including comparisons, historical
constructions, etc., is indispensable to linguistics as well as
developmental psychology and epistemology.

Neither psychology nor linguistics are capable of deducing facts
on an apriori basis and experimental control always remains fundamental. Yet this does not mean that psychology or linguistics can
be satisfied through an empiricist interpretation of the experiments.
As a matter of fact, there exists no observable datum without an
interpretation, given by the subject as well as by the experimenter.
Thus any knowledge consists in a conceptualization of the observed
data and, as a natural consequence, will always entail models. The
model is thus the fundamental tool of knowledge that psychology and
linguistics entail. As an instrument of knowledge, it embodies the
known observables and gives them a more or less necessary structure.
This we have referred to as the process of necessitation derived from
the constructive powers of the observed and observing subject.

There are here two problems, as we stated in a recent article.
(Piaget, 1976). "The first concerns the development of "the real,"
in the sense of an ensemble of recognized "facts" as it relates to
the development of the possible and the necessary. The second is the
problem of the strikingly special status enjoyed by "necessary"
relationship between "possibilities." (p. 11) Thus the enrichment
through discovery whether in the child's development or in that of
sciences, will become more and more integrated at its two poles.
To be more exact, it must increasingly intersect with these two areas.
This does not reduce reality in any way; to the contrary, reality
greatly benefits as a result. On the one hand, transformations of
reality become a sphere of possible transformations with only those
which have been actualized falling into the category of reality.
On the other hand, compositions of these transformations become
necessary, although this does not remove them from the real realm.
Thus knowledge of reality is forever being refined in these two areas,
a fact which makes it even more difficult to reduce such knowledge
to the terms of the preformationist thesis, the basic framework of
Chomsky's epistemology.

By contrast, constructivism is well equipped to deal with the
totality of real facts as well as with the subject's constant
restructuring of these facts as a function of the two spheres of
possibility and necessity.

Our main point is to emphasize that the relationship between
language and thought cannot be conceived without a careful understanding of the epistemology that sustain their interpretation,
specifically the model that embodies their analysis.

J. Bruner, for instance concedes to psychology the right to use linguistic models and not the same right for "logical" models. This seems inconceivable to us because one never observes an intelligence lacking logic even in the case of profound mental alterations as in schizophrenia. A theory of intelligence without logical model is in itself inadequate and that is also what behaviorism has shown in a very forceful way. The clearest proof of the falsity of Bruner's assertion can be found in the fact that there exists a sensorimotor intelligence with structures of orders, of correspondences and intersections and that this intelligence already entails a logical model inherent to the infant himself. These facts also imply a logical model for the psychologist who studies the infant.

The analysis of the underlying structures of thought and reasoning is essential when one understands what we mean by structure, which happens less frequently than one would intuitively believe. It deals essentially with operations and actions that the child can actualize, that is, what he can do as opposed to what he thinks in his conceptualization. A structural analysis is thus fundamental, notably in the analysis of stages, level by level, and in no way excludes a functional analysis which we have all along also taken into consideration.

Concerning the role of language and the symbolic function in the elaboration of structures, we feel that structures are anterior to language. On the other hand, language and the symbolic function play a fundamental role in the conceptualization and the thematisation of structures. This is not only the case in the child but also takes place at every level in the history of science.

For instance, from an epistemological point of view, it is very interesting to observe that the Bourbakis have built their structures through morphisms and categories that they used from an instrumental point of view without yet thematizing them. Further progress consisted precisely in reaching a thematization through a new conceptualization which gave birth to the "theory of categories" of McLane and Eilenberg.

With regard to Chomsky's position, we find it somewhat valid to maintain that the biological basis of language is by itself sufficient to explain it. According to Chomsky, "the literature contains no evidence or argument to support this remarkable factual claim, nor even any explanation of what sense it might have... They (The Geneva School) reject the hypothesis that certain principles of language structures (and other cognitive structures) are "not only present at an extremely early age, but are hereditary." The postulated principles, they insist, are not "preformed" (i.e. governed by genetically determined factors) but rather arise through the child's activity and are explained by "regulatory and autoregulatory mechanisms." These are, however, described in terms so vague that it is hard to know what is intended. (Chomsky, 1976, p. 17-18).

Such does not seem to us to be the case. Any serious biologist knows today the difficulties in problems dealing with cognitive heredity and the neodarwinian theories are today more and more abandoned under the impulse of new facts and interpretations. During the Royaumont Symposium, in 1975, Changeux proposed a compromise between Chomsky's thesis and ours which satisfies us, in maintaining the point of view that, in addition to the action of the genes, the activity plays a fundamental role in the epigenesis. His opening lecture at the College de France is a model of caution and of the reality of the complexity of the problems which remain to be solved. Let us be reminded of the positions of Paul Weiss and Von Furster, among many, which are sufficient to show the adventurous character of the hypothesis of a genetically determined universal grammar.

As to the affirmation that the Geneva School brings no factual evidence concerning the relationship between the sensorimotor intelligence and language, it is enough to refer to the works of Brown, McNeill and H. Sinclair, as well as the very clear article of Inhelder on this subject matter. (Inhelder, 1978). Language is part of a more general cognitive organization with its roots in action and in sensorimotor mechanisms deeper than the linguistic phenomenon. More precisely language is one element in a set of manifestations resting on the semiotic function of which symbolic play, deferred imitation and mental imagery all partake. The fundamental difference between Chomsky and us is that we consider all cognitive acquisitions, including language, to be the outcome of a gradual process of construction starting with the evolutionary forms of biological embryogenesis and ending up with modern scientific ideas. We thus reject the concept of preprogramming in any strict sense. What we consider as innate, however, is the general ability to synthesize the successive levels reached by the increasingly complex cognitive organization.

Thanks to language we observe three major differences between verbal and sensorimotor behavior.

(1) Sensorimotor patterns follow events without really exceeding the speed of the action, whereas verbal patterns by using narration and evocation can represent a long chain of actions very rapidly.

(2) Sensorimotor coordinations are restricted to immediate space and time, whereas language provides to thought the possibility to range over vast stretches of time and space, liberating it from the immediate.

(3) Sensorimotor intelligence proceeds by means of successive acts, step by step. Thought, by contrast, particularly through language, can represent simultaneously all the elements of an organized structure.

Thus language plays an important role from the dual point of view of symbolic condensation as well as social regulation. For this and other reasons we consider the mental representation transcending the here and now as the outcome of sensorimotor intelligence.

According to Chomsky what is hereditary is not the grammar but the conditions of the cognitive and linguistic structures. We are not denying the fact that these structures imply hereditary conditions of functioning. We simply maintain that these necessary conditions are not sufficient. For instance the epistemological thesis that we have come to defend supposes of course the existence of a hereditary functioning of our nervous system, but this in no way means that these ideas were hereditarally preformed since a number of our colleagues (Chomsky among others) who possess the same nervous system do not accept them. Evidently there exist specific hereditary conditions but they serve to the construction of intelligence itself.

As we stated it in a recent article (Piaget, 1975): "Setting aside the problem of highly differentiated instincts, it is hard to see how a new behavior could evolve without some phenotypical trials. It is thus in a collaboration between biology and psychology or ethology that we can expect certain kind of progress in our knowledge" (p. 218). This seems to us to be particularly the case in the development of language. We should add that in the relationship between language and the symbolic function, the latter, which includes mental imagery, deferred imitation, etc., plays a fundamental role in the individual formation of concepts. Language, however, undergoes collective and social regulations providing an interindividual basis and dimension which makes this form of conceptualization much larger than simple sensorimotor outcomes. This leads us to question two.

II. *How is the acquisition and development of language influenced by interpersonal and intrapersonal verbal and nonverbal behavior?*

To begin with it should be remembered that we have essentially dealt from a structural point of view with an "epistemic" subject where the individual differences are not at the center of such analysis. But it should be stressed also that language entails the intervention of interindividual factors to a much greater extent than sensorimotor coordinations or other aspects of the symbolic function. To understand the meaning of intra and interindividual factors it is useful to constrast the types of signifiers that are found in symbolic play and in language. The symbol, which is the main tool of expression found in symbolic play, is a signifier which is different from the object it designates, and yet has some relationship to it. In effect we find symbols which have a conventional or social meaning and symbols which have a meaning only for the individual. In fact since symbols are motivated by the object, they may be created by the child himself and for his use alone. This clearly points to

intrapersonal verbal and nonverbal behavior. The first symbols of
the child's play are individual creations and yet all symbols bear
a nonarbitrary relationship with the objects they designate. This
distinction is important; symbols can be socially shared or they can
be the result of the child's own creativity. Thus the symbol presents
an intermediary situation in two respects. First, its individual or
social meaning places it half in the realm of convention and half in
the realm of the child's individual activity. Second, since the
symbol bears a resemblance to the things signified, it situates itself
in the middle of the process of abstraction. It is neither an indi-
cator or a cue, since it is not part of an object and it is not a
sign. By contrast, language essentially deals with signs, which are
conventional in nature and therefore necessarily collective. They
do not resemble the objects they designate and are essentially
arbitrary. This means that interindividual factors will play a much
greater role in the mastery and the development of language as opposed
to symbolic play.

As we have observed, the acquisition and the development of
language are influenced by interpersonal factors to the extent that
language is an integral part of social interaction, and yet will also
remain confined to an intrapersonal sphere as we observe it in the
case of egocentric speech. This points to the fact that language
cannot be considered alone; that it cannot be detached from the total
context of the symbolic function which entails at least four behavior
patterns which appear almost simultaneously, namely deferred imitation
which starts after the disappearance of the model, symbolic play,
evocative memory and mental imagery.

As to the use of the concept of "epistemic subject," it is
important to keep in mind the context in which this notion arose —
namely the structural characteristics of stages of development and
not the individual behavioral features. Stages deal with normative
characteristics of development; they deal with the description of
behaviors that children have in common at a given moment of their
development and·as such transcend individual differences. This is
not to imply that individual differences are not without importance.
Yet when one deals with structural aspects it is imperative to understand that in observing individual children we are able, through the
use of a concept such as "epistemic subject," to formulate more
precise theoretical tools for the conceptualization of the mechanisms
of knowledge. This has always been out main emphasis.

III. *Are the verbal and nonverbal signal systems interrelated?*

It is clear from what we have already noted that the verbal and
nonverbal signal systems are deeply interrelated. Let us first
examine the situation at the level of the symbolic function. Here
it is clear that language does not stand alone but is part of a number
of other acquisitions that we already mentioned. What we would like

to stress here is the structural aspect of the relationship between
verbal and nonverbal symbolic systems. Mental imagery for instance
transcends language and proceeds from the internalization of deferred
imitation, which points to its ontogenesis. Sensorimotor coordinations are at their source to the same extent that they lead to
language. Thus one can distinguish two types of relationship: horizontal and longitudinal ones. From a longitudinal point of view, it
is important to stress that the sensorimotor development influences
every activity found at the level of the symbolic function, that there
is a functional continuity between this first stage of cognitive
development and the appearance of the symbolic function and yet a
structural discontinuity between the two. To imply that verbal and
nonverbal signal systems are not interrelated would negate the importance of imitation (specifically deferred imitation) in the transition
from sensorimotor intelligence to representational thought.

Representational thought implies the development of a symbolic
function, i.e., the differentiation of signifiers and signified since
it entails the evocation of what is not present, which it can do only
by means of differentiated signifiers. To be sure, at the previous
sensorimotor stages, every behavior makes use of significations
ascribed to objects or to the gestures of others, etc., but the only
signifiers used are perceptual "indices" or conditioned cues, i.e.,
signifiers that are still undifferentiated from what is signified and
thus constitutes merely one of its aspect. A symbolic function, then,
has not yet emerged, if by this is meant the differentiation of signified. But with the birth of representational thought, this differentiation emerges and appears even as a necessary condition of the
representational act as such. Since one of the most specific forms
of differentiated signifiers is the system of verbal signs, one might
assume that the development of representational thought is merely
associated with the acquisition of language. Indeed, as we have
stressed it before, it is self-evident that this is a factor of major
importance. But if language, which is already fully organized within
the social environment and transmitted to the child by education,
does, in fact, play such a role in the development of representational
thought and thought in general, one has not therewith said all, for
two fundamental problems still remain to be resolved. The first is
to understand why language appears neither earlier or later than it
does, i.e., to determine the context in which its acquisition becomes
possible. Conditioning is not a sufficient explanation for it occurs
much earlier. Consequently, we must consider a more precise concept,
i.e., imitation. It remains necessary to determine the form of
imitation that is relevant for there are numerous forms, some of which
also appear much earlier than, and others, concurrently with, the
acquisition of language.

Deferred imitation is the proper link between all aspects of
representational thinking (including language). The second problem
is to determine whether the verbal sign is the only differentiated

signifier implicated or if, in fact, others are also involved in the birth of representational thinking and, if so, whether or not they are contemporaneous with the acquisition of language. As we noted before it is clear that symbols and signs present in the behavioral patterns of representational thinking appear simultaneously. Thus they imply a necessary horizontal relationship as well as common sensorimotor antecedents.

Furthermore, it is noteworthy that deferred imitation leads to the involvement of imitation in all forms of the symbolic function that appear synchronously during the course of the second year. In the Origins of Intelligence in Children (Piaget, 1936/1963), this observation led us to consider imitation as the process that ensures the transition from sensorimotor intelligence or representational thought. Yet well before deferred imitation, from the age of 8-9 months on, sensorimotor imitation clearly testifies to an effort to copy a presented model, for example, in the case of imitation of movements relative to the face of others, without a visible equivalent on the child's own body. This behavior cannot be reduced to simple associative transfers.

In fact, in this context, the problem is ultimately again of an epistemological nature. That is, it involves a distinction between a point of view which implies that knowledge consists essentially in copying reality versus a point of view which we have defended all along, which conceives of knowledge as constructing systems of trans- formations which become progressively adequate. As we have noted elsewhere (Piaget, 1970) "... in order to make a copy we have to know the model we are copying, but according to this theory of knowledge the only way to know the model is by copying it until we are caught in a circle incapable of ever knowing whether our copy of the model is like the model or not." (p. 15) The very fact that verbal and nonverbal signal systems are interrelated at all levels of the devel- opment, except of course during the sensorimotor stage, points to the importance of knowledge as a constant act of active verbal and non- verbal reconstructions and transformations.

IV. *How can one best deal with the issue of nature versus nurture in our attempts to unravel the basic issues in the field of language and cognition?*

   (a) Of what importance is the biological basis of language perception and production?

   (b) Of what importance is the study of individuals who suffer from pathological conditions of language and thought?

The essential problem here is to deal with the interpretation that one can give to phenocopies as the result of actions of the external milieu upon the internal one and as a channel for hereditary

variations through the exigencies of this modified internal milieu.
By phenocopy we mean the replacement of an initial phenotype by a
subsequent genotype presenting the same distinctive characteristics.
In our work Biology and Knowledge (Piaget 1967/1971) we sought to
show the relationship and functional continuity that connect the
process of the formation and development of knowledge to the biological mechanisms of autoregulation peculiar to the organism. In this
essay we attempted to show that one of the most general processes in
the development of cognitive structures consists in the replacement
of exogeneous knowledge by endogeneous reconstructions that reconsti-
tute the same forms but incorporate them into systems whose internal
composition is a prerequisite.

     Let us first recall that all exogeneous knowledge presupposes
an endogeneous framework since it implies an assimilation and not
simply association among perceptions. Assimilation requires assimilative instruments such as setting into relation or into relation or
into correspondence, the attributions of predicates, etc.; these
instruments imply endogeneous frameworks or "forms" even if their
"contents" are exogeneous. Such endogeneous inferences can be applied
to any object whatsoever and can function even without objects as in
"pure" mathematics. Beginning with the cognitive development of the
child and throughout the entire course of the history of scientific
thought, we can observe a more or less continuous pathway from
exogeneous to endogeneous knowledge. This is the nature of the case,
since the general tendency of the mind is to pass beyond empiricism
in the direction of deductive models. But the fundamental problem
is to establish what this pathway consists of.

     There are two possible interpretations: either it can be reduced
to a simply interiorization or else it can be replaced with reconstruction on a new level. The hypothesis of pure interiorization
would not appear here merely for the purpose of admitting that all
mental experience can be interiorized as mental experience; this form
of interiorization goes without saying and we admit it like everyone
else. But we also have always emphasized the fact that all interiorization of action demands a reconstruction on the level of conceptualization. The hypothesis of pure interiorization would further imply
that physical experiences thus interiorized in mental representations
would then be able to acquire the status of logicomathematical
connections; logic and mathematics would thus constitute only a "well-
made language" assuring exogeneous knowledge a seemingly endogeneous
status but by a simple translation of physical properties into
linguistically appropriate expressions. Now it is on this point that
the difficulties arise. The facts suggest that endogeneous knowledge
exhibits autonomous structuration without thereby being reduced to
interiorization of exogeneous contributions, but rather completing
them by reconstructions that go far beyond them and tend to replace
them more or less completely according to the areas involved.

On a biological as well as psychological level, the exogeneous acquisition modifies the field of internal equilibrium of the organism or of the subject. In both cases there is a new and enriching reequilibration due to an endogeneous reconstruction that replaces the exogeneous contribution while reproducing its forms and integrating them in a restructuration of the whole. This is explained not only by the pressures of the milieu but also by the active and internal reactions (scanning, etc.) of the organism or of the subject acting on the milieu, which it modifies and utilizes without limiting itself to submission. These facts point to the complexity of the problem of nature versus nurture in the development of language and cognition. It goes without saying that a concept of hereditability which does not entail active reconstructions through the assimilative instruments of the subject is virtually meaningless. Phenocopy allows us to understand how the actions of the milieu might become hereditary in an indirect way, and in no way presupposes that either intelligence or language are the result of simple hereditary programming.

The study of individuals who suffer from pathological conditions of language and thought is crucial in assessing the relationship between language and thought. More specifically, since language possesses its own logic, one may ask the following question: does this fact constitute not only an essential but the unique factor in the learning of logic? Here psychopathological data will further support what we have previously stated. We have available two sources of important information concerning this subject: first, the comparison of normal children with deaf children, who do not have the attribute of articulate language but possess complete sensorimotor schemes and with blind children who are in the opposite situation. Secondly, the comparison of linguistic progress in the normal child with the development of intellectual operations. The logic of deaf children has been studied by H. Furth (1966), Vincent (1951) and Oléron (1961) among others. What is interesting to note is that when operatory tests are used with deaf children, the results indicate a systematic delay in the appearance of logic in deaf children. Yet one cannot speak of a deficiency as such because the same stages of development as observed in the normal child are encountered, although with a delay of one to two years. It should also be noted that seriation and spatial operations are normal (perhaps a slight delay in the case of the former). The classifications have their usual structures and are only slightly less mobile in response to suggested changes of criteria when compared with normal children. Learning of arithmetics is relatively easy. Problems of conservation which are an index of reversibility, are solved with only a delay of one or two years. The results are as significant in the case of blind children that Hattwell (1964) studied. In her studies the same tests reveal a delay of up to four years or more compared with normal children, even in the case of elementary questions dealing with relationship of order and topological positions. Yet the blind childrens verbal seriations are normal. But it appears that the sensory

disturbance peculiar to those born blind has from the outset hampered
the development of the sensorimotor schemes and slowed down general
coordination. This is to stress that verbal coordinations are not
sufficient to compensate for this delay and action learning is still
necessary before these children develop the capacity for operations
on a level with that of the normal child or the deaf-mute.

As for the relationship between the development of linguistic
and intellectual operations, H. Sinclair has shown a close connection
between the stages of development of seriation and the structure of
the terms used. At the pre-operational level the child understands
the expressions of the higher level only when they are integrated
into orders of assignments, but he does not use them spontaneously.
If the child is trained to use these expressions he will do so with
difficulty and the training seldomly influence his notions of conservation and not more than one case out of ten. Seriation is somewhat
improved by verbal training because then, the linguistic process also
relates to the act of comparison and therefore helps the concept
itself.

These psychopathological data indicate again that language does
not constitute the source of logic but is, on the contrary, structured
by it. In this respect the study of pathological conditions of
language and thought points to the fact that the roots of logic are
to be sought in the general coordination of actions including (as we
have already noted) verbal behavior, beginning with the sensorimotor
level whose schemes are of fundamental importance. This schematism
continues thereafter to develop and to structure thought, even verbal
thought, in terms of the progress of actions, until the construction
of logicomathematical operations.

V.   *Of what importance is the current research in comparative
     psycholinguistics (recent attempts to train chimpanzees and/or
     apes via sign language or any other method)?*

Since we are in no way specialized in this kind of research, we
will restrict our answer to some speculative comments and consider
these attempts within the dual realm of interdisciplinary research
and psychopathological studies.

It is clear that there exists the possibility of a real continuity within the evolutionary spectrum. In genetic epistemology, in
developmental psychology or within the biological range we can never
reach a point where we can say that "here is the beginning of logical
structures." As soon as we start talking about the general coordination of actions, we find ourselves going even further back into the
area of biology.

We also immediately get into the realm of the coordinations
within the nervous system and the neural networks, as discussed, for

instance by McCulloch and Pitts (McCulloch, 1965). And then if we look for the roots of the logic of the nervous system we have to go back a step further. We find basic organic coordinations. If we go further still into the realm of comparative biology, as those comparative psycholinguistic studies do, we find also structures of inclusion, ordering correspondence everywhere. This interdisciplinary framework, which proceeds through regressive analysis can certainly provide the conditions for the emergence of initially surprising results obtained by workers in the field of comparative psycholinguistics. We want to restrict ourselves to psychology and emphasize again that the formation of logical and mathematical structures in human thinking cannot be explained by language alone, but has its roots in the general coordination of actions. In this context training of chimpanzees might lead to conclusions which emphasize the importance of these most general forms of sensorimotor coordinations as indispensable prerequisite to the development of any form of symbolic function.

VI. What are the most important and promising applications of research in the psychology of language and cognition?

Any new theory of cognitive development will necessarily have to be of an interdisplinary nature. This seems to us to be one of the most fruitful yet often misunderstood aspects of research. As we have noted elsewhere (Piaget, 1970b) "interdisciplinary research can result from two sorts of inquiry, one relating to common structures or mechanisms and the other to common methods, although both sorts may of course be involved equally." (p. 9) It is important also that interdisciplinary trends receive a continual impetus, without implying that everyone should be of the same opinion. Within the interdisciplinary framework one usually arrives at three kinds of resolutions of problems which are enriching each particular field of research. These solutions are: (1) reduction from the "higher" to the "lower" (2) irreductibility of the phenomenon of the "higher" level and (3) assimilation by partial reduction of the "higher" but also by enrichment of the "lower" by the "higher." It is in the development of explanations that the most useful and promising aspect can probably be found. Outside of methodological problems which are inherent to an area of research and not necessarily appropriate to another, interpretations which are sustained by interdisciplinary considerations tend to be richer than when they remain limited to a particular field of inquiry.

Within the context of this discussion, the links between linguistics and logic are of unquestioned importance and are still in process of full development, particularly as they have an impact upon longstanding arguments between psychologists and sociologists. This it should be noted is no accident. The convergence of a linguistic doctrine like F. de Saussure's and a sociological theory like Durkheim's is quite remarkable: language as we have noted it is a collective "institution" transmitted from the outside and imposing itself upon individuals. Yet, in the context of inter-disciplinary research, one should note that any innovation which is made must accord with common rules established before, and their initiatives must be subject to the approval of the linguistic group, which may reject or accept them, but in the latter case only because of needs related to the overall equilibrium of the system. Durkheim drew from his ideas on the social totality the conclusion that the rules of logic are imposed by the group upon the individual, in particular through language, the shaper of intelligence and the holder of structures which are imposed from childhood through education. This is of course not our interpretation. Although it is true that language consists in a set of collective signs it does not follow that they are imposed as such upon the individual. On the contrary. Yet it precisely through interdisciplinary inquiries and analysis of this type that conclusions and interpretations which go beyond a particular realm of intellectual functioning can be arrived at.

The social and human sciences have their own series of epistemo-logical problems. But there are two distinct types of questions to be considered in this connection: questions concerning the research worker as such, or, in other words, those that are proper to the epistemology of his branch of study as a particular form of scientific knowledge; and those that concern the subject of study himself, who, since he is a human being, is a source of knowledge — whether artistic, technical, scientific, etc. — available to the various societies which is the origin of the human sciences. By grouping interdisciplinary problems around realities — structures or rules, values and meanings — that are common to them all, we have referred to the manifestations of the activity of a natural subject. It remains for us to see how the human sciences regard this subject as a subject, for this is perhaps one of the most promising points of convergence to be kept in mind for the future, although it has not yet been analysed sufficiently.

VII. *Do you feel that the field of language and cognition is, as some believe, in a state of transition searching for a new theory or paradigm? If so, what kind of theory do you believe will emerge or is at present emerging?*

Let us reiterate what we have stated in the previous question. Any new theory that will emerge in the field of language and cognition will by necessity be of an interdisciplinary nature, but in many ways a healthy state of any theory is to be always in transition. For instance, we are constantly revising our own point of view in light of new facts and data which emerge not only from the field of cognition but also and often in a major form in other areas of science. For instance it is clear that cybernetics brought major revisions to our own concepts. As one of us observed (Voyat, 1977) ... "we should note that work on artificial intelligence bears the

deep imprint of Piaget's influence." (p. 347) Yet it should be
stressed that this influence was reciprocal. The conceptual link
with cybernetics was also established thanks to the concepts of
regulation and self regulation — i.e. the intrinsic conceptual
components of the notion of structure. Cybernetics is only one
example but it is representative of the destiny of any real scientific
theory: it constantly moves towards new levels of equilibrium and is
never satisfied by its previous accomplishments, for what needs to
be explained is the development of knowledge and knowledge is itself
in constant dialectical development.

The same holds for a specific paradigm which encompasses a
theory. Even more so since the paradigm is the most fragile and yet
the most important framework of a theory. What can be said about a
theory can also be said about a paradigm because there is an intrinsic
relationship between the two. The accumulation of facts or the
elaboration of a theory is in itself not sufficient to lead to new
constructions. Revisions take place constantly at the most abstract
and implicit level of the paradigm, at the level of the interpretation
as well as at the level of the theory and the accumulation of facts.
It is important to understand that the word "transition" describes
this constant state of development which any scientific theory should
undergo, because a theory's creative aspect precisely derives from
the duality between an equilibrium which seems satisfying for a while;
and its perturbation which is essential for its survival.

DIALOGUE IV

Ulric Neisser's Views on the
Psychology of Language and Thought

Ulric Neisser is the Susan Linn Sage Professor of Psychology at Cornell University in Ithaca, New York. He was educated at Harvard, Swarthmore, and M.I.T., receiving the Ph.D. in psychology from Harvard in 1956. He taught at Brandeis University and the University of Pennsylvania before joining the faculty at Cornell in 1967. He served as a Fellow of the Center for Advanced Study in the Behavioral Sciences at Stanford in 1973-74, and as Visiting Sloan Fellow at the University of Pennsylvania in 1980-81. The author of about 60 articles on perception, attention, memory, intelligence, and related topics, he is best known for his books: Cognitive Psychology (1967), Cognition and Reality (1976), and Memory Observed: Remembering in Natural Contexts (1982).

Dialogue IV. Ulric Neisser's Views on the Psychology of Language and Thought

RIEBER: This is an interview with Dr. Neisser. The first question is what role cognition plays in the acquisition and development of language.

NEISSER: I think that at the beginning they are completely interwoven. The infant starts out embedded in a world of objects and events, some of which involve communication. I do think it likely that the baby can distinguish a domain of "communicative actions" from the first. People pick him up, gesture with their hands, and change their facial expressions; they also make what are called "articulatory gestures" with their mouths and throats. That is, they speak. Probably the baby makes no distinction between speech and the other expressive gestures at first. In one case most of the relevant information is auditory while in the other it is mostly visual, but that is not an essential difference. (In the case of sign language, all the linguistic information is visual). More important that the distinction between modalities is the difference between two kinds of "meaning" that are conveyed. On the one hand, there is information about the speaker: about his or her activities, intentions, and feelings. On the other hand there is information about other things; the real linguistic meaning of what is said. The speaker is talking about something, usually something close at hand. The infant's understanding of the referential use of language, and of linguistic structure, surely matures later than his understanding of its expressive function.

Let me go back to your question again and try to answer it explicitly. For both kinds of meaning, cognition must come first. I think infants perceive people — separate, animate individuals — from the beginning. It is those people, already perceived and —

123

in a sense — understood, whose intentions and feelings are conveyed by their expressive gestures. Similarly, understanding what is being said about a particular object depends on being able to perceive the object in the first place. At first, the understanding is closely integrated with perception itself. Vygotsky (1962) has a very interesting discussion of this. He points out that for the young child an object's name is an integral part of it. Even older children do not agree that names can be arbitrarily altered. When Vygotsky asked children if you could call a cow "ink" or ink "cow," they rejected this possibility indignantly. "Ink is used for writing." It is almost as if names were perceptible aspects of objects: sound patterns that one frequently perceives just when the object is present. Not always, of course, but then most properties are only intermittently perceived.

RIEBER: I think it was Cassirer who said that the name of an object called that object into being. Before a thing is labelled one cannot really say that it exists in the full sense of the word, although the cognition may be there before. How do you feel about that?

NEISSER: Maybe Cassirer means that objects exist "in the full sense of the word" only when people have philosphical discussions about them. In any ordinary or reasonable sense, he must be wrong. The preverbal child knows perfectly well that things exist. He knows that objects differ from one another; he can classify them, handle them, do things with them be sorry if they break. He is interested in all these aspects of things long before he has names for them. So are animals, for that matter.

RIEBER: How would you feel about the development of a concept of self? It is relatively easy to deal with all of this in talking only about external objects in the world, but how would your ideas relate to the concept of oneself?

NEISSER: That is a more difficult question. The full-fledged concept of self emerges only very gradually. Indeed, it continues to develop even in adulthood: that's one of the things people work on during psychotherapy. There is no day when we can draw a line and say "until now Junior had no sense of self, but today he has one." More over I believe, contrary to the generally accepted view, that concepts about other people develop earlier than the concept of self. Others are more obviously perceptible. Their emotions and intentions are easily seen and heard; one's own emotions and intentions are more subtly specified and may be harder to perceive. Sometimes, though, the concept is defined in temporal terms: to have a concept of self is to think of oneself as an individual who has a particular past and potential future. That criterion is surely not met until after the child understands a good deal of language. The past and the future are frequent topics of conversation almost everywhere; without language, it is hard to see how they could come into awareness in any significant way.

RIEBER: I think in fairness to Cassirer, that is part of what he was talking about. I think he was talking about the names, rather than anything else. How much do we know about preverbal cognition? When the child has some cognitive understanding of an object, yet no word for it or no ability to express the word for it?

NEISSER: One way of approaching that problem is to consider the results of animal experimentation. Animals don't have words, but they manage to do intricate and complicated things. That's one direct demonstration of what is possible without language.

RIEBER: Yes, but are animals really doing the same things that kids are doing?

NEISSER: Nobody is ever really doing the same thing as anybody else. Everyone is embedded in their own particular situation. Animals are not doing the same things kids do; you are not doing the same thing that I do. Each of us is unique. Although there is a larger gulf that separates people from animals, we mustn't get trapped by questions like "Is it the same thing?"

RIEBER: Is it comparable in the sense that you can make the jump in analogy?

NEISSER: I think analogy is sometimes appropriate; we know that both animals and children remember things, solve detour problems, go back and get things they left behind, classify appropriately, and so on. Their mental life is not what yours would be in the same situation, but in many cases they can achieve similar results.

RIEBER: Even though the animal is formally taught to do it and the child is not?

NEISSER: You're right about the importance of that difference, but we are thinking about different examples of animal behavior. The examples I had in mind were relatively simple ones: solving detour problems, reaching through the bars of a cage with a stick to get a banana that would be otherwise out of reach. Those are clear cases of realistic and entirely nonverbal thinking, so they are relevant to the claim that only language can give understanding. I think they refute that claim. Nevertheless it is certainly true that a skill learned in the context of human culture is entirely different from one acquired by isolated and painstaking instruction.

RIEBER: Clearly your position, which is not very radical at all today, is that cognition comes first and lays the groundwork for verbal behavior.

NEISSER: One particularly striking example of cognition coming first, based not on developmental but on cross-cultural studies, is the work that Eleanor Rosch did in New Guinea (Heider, 1972). She studied a people who have no distinguishing names for colors at all, whose color vocabulary is restricted to one word for "light" and another for "dark." Despite this limited vocabulary, the Dani classify colors much as we do when they exhibit the same patterns of difficulty in remembering colors, and so on.

RIEBER: How do you feel about the existence of discrete, linear stages of cognitive development and their relationship to linguistic behavior? Do you think there are discrete stages?

NEISSER: Those issues are much more complicated than Piaget at first believed. It is true that for any given task, you can see cognitive skills emerging later that were not present before. At one time a child does not know how to find hidden objects at all, later he can find them under favorable circumstances, still later he can find them even when the experimenter shifts them around in tricky ways. I am sure that these skills are influenced by accumulated experience, though the child must know how to use that experience. Whether the development will appear to exhibit discrete "stages" will depend on the particulars of the experience in question. What Piaget called "thinking in formal operations," for example, apparently does not occur except in children who have had the benefit of a good deal of education, and not even always then. Studies of cognitive development conducted in Europe and America invariably confound age and education: all the ten-year-olds have been in school for five years. We know relatively little about the course of cognitive development after the fifth year of life that is independent of the systematic effect of schooling.

RIEBER: You apparently never will, the way this culture is going in schooling. It is important to imagine a child not subjected to it. I suppose that's why there is so much fascination with the Wild Boy (see, eg. Lane).

NEISSER: One does not know what to make of the few cases like that. A child brought up outside of culture is in a very unnatural situation — even more unnatural than one finds in the laboratories of experimental psychology. Humanity has evolved in culture, not outside of it; people are not genetically adapted to growing up alone. But controlling for the effects of schooling does not require the study of feral children. There are still places in the world where children don't go to school. I think that the cross-cultural study of development is one of the last great resources of cognitive psychology: an untapped source of data that we are just beginning to appreciate. It is not too late to use it in order to get some perspective on ourselves. We need it urgently. Most psychological research has been restricted to a particular social class in a

particular kind of society. Anything that will provide a different
point of view is very important. There are several sources of new
perspectives: not only cross-cultural research but the study of
infancy, the research on animals, and the exploration in artificial
intelligence.

RIEBER: Would you put them in that order of importance?

NEISSER: I am not sure. Each of them has already contributed
something. There have been some very exciting studies of infant
perception lately; there are some slowly emerging insights about the
essentials of thinking from the artificial intelligence work; the
attempts to teach language to apes should tell us something; and there
has been a little bit of well-conducted cross-cultural research in
cognition. The last is the most difficult to do well, for political
reasons among others, but in the end I think it would be very reward-
ing.

Let's return to the acquisition of language. The infant doesn't
just learn the names of things, of course — that's hardly language
at all. He discovers the structure of language as well.

RIEBER: I notice you put it in terms of discovery rather than
of having it a priori.

NEISSER: Yes, but discovery requires a prepared mind, an appro-
piate anticipatory schema. That applies to discovery in science and
in interpersonal relations as well as to what I loosely called the
discovery of the structure of language. The question is how much
preparation, and of what kind, does the child have for language?
There may be a great deal.

RIEBER: Does the child perceive the structure of language by
engaging in its function, that is, by talking himself?

NEISSER: I don't think so, though production must play a large
role when it occurs. Nevertheless, comprehension seems to come before
production in many cases. In second-language learning we can generally understand more than we can say, and I believe that is true of
children with their first language as well. Lenneberg (1967) interviewed a child who never spoke at all and yet understood a great deal.

RIEBER: Lenneberg was referring to an autistic child with whom
he had worked, who allegedly had never spoken; at least no one had
ever heard him speak. I've seen such children myself over the years.
My feeling is that nevertheless they silently talk to themselves,
because it is safer to do so.

NEISSER: You may be right about the children you have observed.
In general, though, one need not actually perform meaningful

movements in order to perceive and understand them. Let me explain this with an analogy between speaking and dancing. A dancer moves; a person watching the dance picks up information about the movements from what Gibson (1966) calls the optic array. That is, the optical patterns available to the viewer's eye specify the movements that the dancer has made. Similarly a speaker executes movements in his mouth and throat; the listener then picks up information about those movements from what we might call the acoustic array. The sound patterns available to the listener's ear specify the articulatory movements of the speaker. The English language obscures this parallel by allowing us to talk about "hearing sounds" when we listen to a speaker but making it unnatural to say we "see lights" when we watch the dancer. Nevertheless the situations are closely analogous. We pick up information from the light that specifies how the dancer is moving, and what the dance means; we pick up information from the sound that specifies how the speaker is moving his articulators, and what those movements mean. (There is also some visual information for the articulatory movements, just as there is some acoustic information for the movements of the dancer, but I don't want to get into those questions here).

No one would suppose that a person must have been a dancer himself in order to appreciate the ballet. When, then, would we think a person must have been a speaker himself in order to understand speech? To be sure, experience with producing the movements makes some difference: a skilled dancer watching the ballet will notice things that a non-dancer might not see, and may come away with a more accurate notion of what happened. Nevertheless, even the non-dancer can understand a good deal of it. Similarly, an experienced speaker will listen to speech differently than a person who has never talked, and may understand more of it, but even a non-speaker may get a great deal of meaning from what he hears.

RIEBER: Yes, but these two situations may be very different. Perception of language, which involves the agreed-upon meanings of words, is on a very different level of abstraction than perceiving the emotional meaning of the movements of a dancer.

NEISSER: Of course language is subtler in many ways: it has semantic content, makes reference, obeys grammatical rules. I don't want to minimize its special qualities, but the sheer experience of speaking may not be relevant for them. Self-production is surely not necessary to understand semantic meaning, for example. We understand the meanings of all kinds of signals that we can't produce; even animals do.

My argument does not mean that speech perception just "happens," without any activity on the listener's part. Continuous activity is required to perceive speech, or dancing, or any other structured event. The perceiver continually develops schematic anticipations

of what will come next, and modifies them from moment to moment as
the event proceeds. Nobody could perceive speech who didn't engage
himself actively with it. In fact, I can go further. In my view, the
experiences that people call "mental images" are really structured
anticipations of information. (See Cognition and Reality, 1976,
Chapter 7.) It follows, I think, that you couldn't perceive speech
unless you could imagine it.

RIEBER: That's a kind of perception.

NEISSER: It's a prerequisite for perception, and it's also a
kind of production. You really can't perceive much of anything without being able to imagine it, at least schematically.

RIEBER: That's an important idea that has not been considered
very often: the imaginative power one must have in order to engage
in anything.

NEISSER: It is necessary in perceiving any complex event that
takes place over time. To follow something that is happening —
speech or dancing, in my examples — you must be able to anticipate
the kind of information that will appear next. If the event should
stop in midflight, as when the telephone connection is broken or the
lights go out in the ballet theatre, you find yourself imagining what
the next few moments would have brought. That is, you have a mental
image of it.

RIEBER: It's like picturing your schema.

NEISSER: I'm not very comfortable with the notion of "picturing." You don't first have the schema and then look at it; you just
execute it, and that execution is "having the image."

RIEBER: Let's center in on the nature/nurture question now.
How do you feel about the perennial circle? It's been with us since
the beginning.

NEISSER: At one level, the problem can be dismissed with a
platitude. Everyone knows that what really happens is an interaction.
There is an initial nervous system, and an environment. They continually and reciprocally shape one another from the beginning (that is,
from conception), and so you cannot attribute any particular thing
a person does to nature or to nurture alone. The issue becomes
clearer when we consider a range of possibilities rather than an
individual outcome. We are impressed with "nature" — that is, with
genetic endowment — if a species does the same sort of things over
a wide range of environments. Similarly, we are impressed with
"nurture" when different species can be made to react similarly by
closely controlling the environment.

One of the most impressive pieces of research on the nature side in recent years is the study of congenitally deaf children conducted by Feldman, Goldin-Meadow, and Gleitman (1978). These children were born deaf to hearing parents. Because of the peculiar politics of the deaf establishment in this country, the parents were warned not to teach or encourage sign language in their children. Nevertheless, each of the children spontaneously invented a rudimentary sign language themselves. Their gestures were organized into the equiv- alent of at least two-word sentences; in some cases much longer ones. Thus it is clear that language is, so to speak, "more innate" than we might have thought; children produce structured referential sequences of signs even in the absence of an encouragement from the environment. (It is also clear that language is less specifically dependent on speech and sound than we might have thought — less than I thought, for that matter. Cognition and Reality, 1976, makes some casual remarks about a supposedly necessary link between language and sound that I now regret). Of course there were limits to what these children achieved, but then they were in a very limited environment: nobody was answering them.

It seemed for a while as if there might be equally striking findings on the nurture side in the Gardners' work with their chimpanzee "Washoe." Washoe learned to make a considerable number of signs adopted from American Sign Language, and other apes have done the same since. But knowing how to use a number of signs is still a long way from having acquired language itself. (More recent works by Terrace (1979) and by Seidenberg and Petitto (1979) have shown that the signing apes do not use ASL and do not have language in any reasonable sense of the term. Their failure to acquire language, even with the expenditure of so much effort, actually adds more weight to the "nature" side of the debate).

RIEBER: Let's return to the thing you mentioned before — how nature and nurture interact. Certainly we can't attribute it entirely to one or the other, but can we describe just how they interact to produce cognition?

NEISSER: I think that the research on that problem is only just beginning. Many of the answers are to be found by studying infancy, and the very early stages of cognition and language. We are just starting to do that. I shouldn't say "we" as if I were personally involved, of course; I have done very little infant research. But many psychologists — T. G. R. Bower and Eleanor Gibson and Peter Eimas and others — have already made important discoveries about infant perception, even speech perception.

One interesting piece of work that is on my mind at the moment is being done by a couple of graduate students at Cornell (Hilke & Clark, 1978). They have been looking at eight-month-old babies engaged in solving Piagetian object-constancy problems. The babies

make sounds — they vocalize — just exactly at points where they
find the problem difficult. There may be a natural link between
cognition and vocalization in humans. Surely another ten or twenty
years of research on infancy will turn up many more such observations.
When we put them together with cross-cultural studies, and with what
we learn from animal studies, we will begin to have some perspective
on the nature-nurture problem.

RIEBER: If an infant vocalizes differently when he is having
some success, as compared to when he is encountering failure, can we
assume that he is experiencing different feelings? Do the different
vocalizations express different feelings?

NEISSER: That is one of the roots of language. So far we have
talked only about language that describes external events, but
language has many other functions and comes from other roots as well.

RIEBER: I think you have made this point quite clear in your
book (Neisser, 1976): that we must not overlook feelings as an important element in giving rise to language and cognition.

NEISSER: Yes.

RIEBER: We have almost systematically ignored it for a long
period of time. Emotions and feelings were unscientific — not to
be investigated.

NEISSER: The only definition of emotion that we have so far is
a very unsatisfactory one: casual reference to our own mental state.
It is hard to go very far with that. There have been attempts to
build a psychology of emotions on a physiological basis instead, but
they have not worked well.

RIEBER: We are going into a period when a tremendous amount of
interest is being focused on the physiological basis of language and
cognition. Many people believe that language and cognition have their
roots in sub-cortical areas of the brain that are associated with
emotions. A lot of basic research is coming out of that hypothesis.
It is an attempt to bridge the gap between the mind and the body.

NEISSER: I don't want to speculate on the functions of different
parts of the brain. It is clear, though, that emotion and communication are related. All the social animals communicate, and some of
the main things they signal to one another are what they intend to
do next: fight, flee, submit, engage in sexual behavior. It is not
unreasonable to call these intentions their "emotions." They are
signalled by gestures and movements of every kind. It would be
remarkable if the same thing were not true of human beings. There
is a good deal of evidence for it; in the cross-cultural study of
facial expression, for example.

These emotional signals are a form of communication for which
we are biologically equipped. I am sure that it is one of the roots
of language. A human being who happened to be born without that
neural equipment, who could not perceive what others do as signifying
their intentions, would be severely handicapped in his use of
language. I have occasionally speculated that this may be what is
the matter with autistic children. They don't seem to perceive the
expressive signs of other people as emotional signals, and are equally
indifferent to embraces and to loving words. As a result, they don't
think of <u>themselves</u> as having emotions or intentions either. They
don't see us as human, in the emotional sense, and don't see themselves as human either. So they seem somewhat inhuman and peculiar
to the observer.

That is just a wild speculation. There is evidently something
amiss in the autistic child's sense of self and others, but it could
originate in various ways. One interesting observation on the sense
of self has recently been made by Gallup (1977) with chimpanzees.
It is another example of what we can learn about nature and nurture
from animal experiments. He begins by putting a mirror in the
chimpanzee's cage for a couple of weeks. Such a chimp spends a lot
of time looking at his reflection, but does he know that it is himself? To find out, Gallup briefly anesthetizes the chimp and paints
a red spot on his forehead. By and by, after he has awakened, the
chimp happens to look in the mirror. Ugh! He strikes himself on
the forehead and begins scratching at the spot! He must know, therefore, that the chimpanzee in the mirror is him. Gallup has never
found this behavior with monkeys. They are interested in the mirrored
reflection too, but they don't seem to know that they are looking at
themselves.

A more recent experiment is even more interesting. Gallup
raised chimpanzees in isolation, so they never saw any other members
of their own species. When they had reached maturity, they were
given the mirror test. These isolation-reared chimpanzees did <u>not</u>
recognize themselves in the mirror. So there are at least two
prerequisites for self-recognition in a mirror: the right kind of
nervous system (monkeys don't do it), and a certain amount of social
experience. It's worth noting, too, that neither of these prerequisites involves language.

Gallup's experiments make a case for both nature and nurture,
but probably neither one is absolute in its effects. Perhaps someone
as ingenious as David Premack would be able to take a monkey (who
doesn't spontaneously recognize himself in mirrors) and teach him
about it. After all, the same optical information is available to
the chimp who succeeds as to the monkey who fails: a certain synchrony
between observer's movements and those of the mirrored animal whom
he is observing. The ability to pick up this information must be a
byproduct of something else; I can't imagine that it has any adaptive

value in its own right. What contribution to survival in the wild
could mirror-recognition make? So we do not know what the origins
of this kind of self-recognition are, or how it might by brought
about.

RIEBER: There is surely more than this to the epistemological
question of self-knowledge. The term "self" is the key here: in human
beings it refers to a system that is far more complex than recognizing
a spot on your head. Chimps are capable of a rudimentary level of
abstraction — they can see the reflection, and identify it, and
identify the spot as being on themselves — but that is very far from
having a self-concept. In that sense, this experiment needs not
disturb those who believe that there is a wide gulf between the animal
and ourselves.

NEISSER: Yes, of course. I wasn't using this example to show
that there is no gulf between man and animal. On the contrary, it
shows that there is a gulf — in this case, between normal chimps and
chimps reared in isolation.

RIEBER: Just as there is a gulf between normally raised children
and children raised in isolation.

NEISSER: But also a gulf between chimp and monkey. That one
is presumably innate, due to "nature," whereas the differences that
derive from different types of rearing are due to "nurture." In this
case both "gulfs" seem to function in much the same way, at least by
this particular measure.

What you say about the human sense of self is true, but we should
realize that there is no such thing as a sharply defined "sense of
self" that all people have and all animals lack. I think I mentioned
this before. It is perfectly reasonable to say that a five-year-old
does not have as clear a sense of self as a twenty-year-old. It is
also reasonable to say that a patient has a better sense of self after
a successful psychoanalysis than he did before. Every individual is
an infinitely complex object, about which it is impossible to know
everything. Therefore there are indefinitely many levels and levels
of self-knowledge. Gallup's experiment shows that the chimpanzee
achieves at least one of those levels, and it's not a trivial one.
Incidentally, we are still far from understanding the experiment
completely. We don't know whether the pre-exposure to the mirror was
responsible for the self-concept that was later tested, for example.
We also can't be sure whether it is a lack of self-concept that
causes monkeys to fail. Perhaps their failure is due to something
less interesting — an obscure sort of visual deficit, for example.

RIEBER: Hasn't Premack found that a chimpanzee will shriek with
horror when he sees a death mask? That would also indicate an awareness of self.

NEISSER: Hebb (1946) made that observation many years ago.
He pointed out that chimps have an apparently innate fear of masks
of every kind, and of anything that looks like a severed head. It's
a difficult observation to interpret. The severed head may not imply
anything deep and philosophical about death to them; they may not
know why they fear it. Many people are mortally afraid of snakes and
don't know the reason why. Their fear doesn't have much cognitive
content.

RIEBER: While we are talking about the apes, do you want to
say any more about the recent attempts to teach sign language or other
languages to them?

NEISSER: I think we will learn a lot. Whether they succeed or
fail, we will get some perspective on what it means to be human that
we don't have now. The work should not be seen as exclusively about
language. Premack (1976), for example, regards himself primarily as
a psychologist studying the nature of thought. His work enables us
to see whether and how various kinds of thinking depend on various
linguistic skills. His subject Sarah seems to understand cause and
effect fairly well: she can produce a string of symbols telling you
that knives are used for cutting apples in half. The concept of
causality, in that limited sense, apparently does not depend on the
special subtleties of human language. That's only one example; there
are many others, and more will come.

The point is not to deny that human language is something
special. Of course it is. There are the kinds of sentences people
make, and the things they talk about, and the cultural matrix in
which they live. I believe that there certainly are genetic differences between people and chimpanzees relevant to language. The fact
that chimpanzees don't invent sign language the way the deaf children
do in the study I mentioned earlier is one proof of that. But we
are very far from understanding what the human endowment is, or what
role it plays in cognition generally. The chimpanzee-language studies
should help to clarify that.

RIEBER: Did you see the recent article in the New York Times
Magazine called Beauty and the Beast? It was about teaching
a gorilla to use language, and the legal complications that arose
because of it. One lawyer claimed that the gorilla had been given
a level of consciousness comparable to man, and therefore had human
rights.

NEISSER: It's my impression that the gorilla experiment has
not been very successful. In any case, rights and laws grow out of
human cultural institutions, not out of experiments with gorillas.
If we should ever encounter other species that have cultural institutions (as the science-fiction writers predict), we will have to
adapt our conception of rights and laws to incorporate them. The

mere possibility of such an encounter, though, can't be taken
seriously as the basis for action. Rights are existential; they come
into being only in concrete contexts. So far, we don't have to take
the problem of the gorilla seriously.

RIEBER: In many ways the problem is related to another issue
that was all over the media last year: the legal definition of death.
Isn't that related to the intellectual definition of life in man?

NEISSER: These are logic-chopping questions for lawyers.
Americans are the most litigious people in the world; they love to
take things to court. New challenges to the legal mind are not
necessarily psychological questions. The psychological concepts of
"life" and "death" are very important, but they don't map comfortably
onto the yes/no distinction that judges are sometimes asked to make.

RIEBER: What are the most important and promising directions
of research on the psychology of language and cognition?

NEISSER: We've covered many of them already, but there are
several others to talk about. One of them is cross-cultural research,
which I mentioned before but didn't elaborate. I think it has a
critical role to play in understanding cognitive development. At
present, we simply don't know whether the development that we observe
and theorize about is the result of maturation, applying to all children, or if it is the result of the formal schooling that our experimental subjects have undergone. The stage of concrete operations
that Piaget describes, for example, may not be a necessary part of
growing up but a consequence of the thousand hours a year that most
children spend in the school environment. The only way to find out
is to study children who don't go to school. Some work of this kind
is being done, and yielding interesting insights.

RIEBER: What exactly is your hypothesis? What does school
provide that just growing up in culture does not provide?

NEISSER: Systematization of knowledge is one thing. The conception that knowledge comes in separable domains, that there are
abstract skills of thought applicable to more than one concrete
problem, that you can get something right without understanding it
and understand it without getting it right. Also, that a major way
to acquire knowledge is to engage in activity that seems meaningless
in its own right, because the teacher asks you to, and that this
activity may have important consequences for you years later.
Scribner and Cole (1973) have written a stimulating paper on this.

RIEBER: That's school and culture coming together to make a
unified way of life. Can you separate schooling and culture?

NEISSER: I'll try to be more systematic. One of the major
things that school does is that it teaches you to read and write:
it makes you literate. That expands your intellectual possibilities
enormously.

RIEBER: Isn't there the possibility that in some cultures people
learn a written language without a formal school, by tutoring as it
were?

NEISSER: Yes, that actually happens in some places. Goody,
Cole and Scribner (1977) have been studying indigenous written
language in Liberia, the Vai script, which many unschooled individuals
know and use for various purposes. It will be interesting to see what
the cognitive consequences of that kind of literacy turn out to be.

Another major consequence of going to school is something that
I can only call the abstract discipline of the school setting. What
we define as "intellectual" in school is remote from practical application, from personal relationships, and from ongoing activity. For
the most part school work is not meaningful in the present; its
importance lies only in the future rewards that are promised to the
educated. The process has powerful effects. Many children in Africa
go to schools that we would consider absolutely terrible: the teachers
themselves are poorly educated, there are few resources like paper
or pencils or books, the principal method of instruction is the rote
memorization of relatively meaningless material. Nevertheless, children who attend these schools for a few years produce very different
patterns of performance than unschooled control children from the
same cultural group.

The cognitive changes produced by schooling and technology seem
to happen very fast. Luria (1977) has an interesting account of
research that he did with Vygotsky in the 1920s, when the peasants
in the Eastern Soviet Union were being collectivized. Six months on
a modern institution like a collective farm seemed to produce tremendous changes in styles of thought. At present we don't know to what
extent these changes are due to the situational and social characteristics of schooling and to what extent they depend on what you
actually learn there, but at least we can pose the problem. That's
great advance. I believe that additional cross-cultural research
will continue to provide ideas relevant to the questions of nature
and nurture. These are old questions, but now we are in a position
to learn something new about them. Learning something new tends to
have a shattering effect on one's thinking. (That's an effect of
schooling too, of course). I am enough of a believer in science, or
empiricism, to think that at certain points there is no substitute
for getting some new facts to think about.

RIEBER: Right, we have been in a rut, no question about it.
We have been entrenched in a narrow framework that stifles the

creative imagination. Do you feel that the field of language and
cognition is, as some believe, in a state of transition searching
for a new theory or paradigm? If so, what kind of theory do you
believe will emerge or is at present emerging?

NEISSER: It certainly is in transition and moving around.
We've just been through a brief period of infatuation with models of
grammar and syntax. They have turned out not to provide as much
guidance for psychologists as had been hoped. We want to understand
the development of language and thought, and the way that speech is
ordinarily understood and used. The first generation of formal
grammars didn't help much in that respect.

RIEBER: Except to tell us what we couldn't find out. It was
a dead end.

NEISSER: It was worth exploring, I think; you don't know how
things will work until you try them. Edison tried thousands of
materials that didn't work before he got the light bulb to glow
properly. More recently, we are trying different directions: case
grammars, semantically based accounts of language, and there is a new
interest in pragmatics: on the actual functions of linguistic utterances and the purposes that the speaker has in mind. It's too early
to know what these new trends will contribute.

RIEBER: One trend that is very popular in developmental psycholinguistics is the study of mother-infant and mother-family-infant
interaction. What is your reaction to it?

NEISSER: Very positive. It is entirely reasonable to study
language in the context where it naturally occurs. That is almost
invariably in a social context, and for young children that means in
the family. Perhaps it's odd that anyone ever thought of studying
language any other way. The same point can be made not only for
language but for cognitive processes in general. For too long we
have been studying cognition in rather artificial laboratory settings.
One can learn things that way, but there comes a time when it is
better to move back and get a better idea of what happens in ordinary
life.

RIEBER: Do you think the new paradigms will be more interpersonal?

NEISSER: They will be more bound to context. That will make
them interpersonal to a considerable extent, though not exclusively.
We may go back to doing the kind of work that Vygotsky (1962) did long
ago, watching the child's spontaneous use of language as he tried to
solve a problem. That led to the notion of internalization of speech;
the children talked to themselves when the problem became difficult,
just as the infants do in Hilke and Clark's study at Cornell. That's
not an interpersonal use of language, but it's a genuine one.

RIEBER: How do you feel about the possibility of a better mind/
body paradigm? By body, I really mean the brain.

NEISSER: There is no doubt that neuropsychology is making great
strides. We know much more now about how the brain works and about
what happens in the brain while cognitive processes are taking place.
Unfortunately, nothing that has been learned so far seems to help
very much with the problems of cognition. Maybe it will in the
future: we will see. My guess is, though, that neuropsychology won't
help very much until we have a better idea of what it can be expected
to explain. We need a clear conception of how language is acquired,
of what goes on in problem solving and how it depends on experience
and culture, if we are to set the right problems for the brain
sciences. Of course, there may be an interactive gain: their discoveries may help to sharpen our concepts, and vice versa.

RIEBER: It seems to me that what we want to discover is how the
two sides of the coin are related; how the nature or capacity that
you are born with, neurologically, facilitates your cognitive and
linguistic ability. In other words, there is a reciprocal relation
between the two sides of the coin, the body and the mind. As you
mature and learn you are changing your brain. You were born with a
capacity that enables you to do something with your brain, and that
is what I think the neuropsychologists have to deal with: to find out
for us how these two things come together.

NEISSER: But the brain is no less complicated than the world.
There is an immensely complex system of millions of neurons, of
chemical transmitters and electrical activity. We need a conceptualization of it. It's not enough to divide the brain into areas,
with this area more important for X and that one for Y; we need to
know how it works. There is not much chance of that in neuropsychology until we have a conception of language and thought that
will suggest what kind of structure one should look for. Without
that, there will be as many alternative models of the complexities
of the brain as we already have of the complexities of the world
around us.

I'll give you an example of what I mean. Some fifteen or twenty
years ago, a rudimentary filter theory of attention was very popular
among psychologists. The idea was that unattended inputs were
filtered out by special peripheral mechanisms, so that only attended
inputs reached higher centers. When a person was attending to visual
stimulation, a sort of "gate" closed against impulses from the ear.
Given that theory of attention, it seemed reasonable to look for
specific filter mechanisms in the nervous system. You probably know
the famous experiment by Hernandez-Peon and his collaborators (1956),
which seemed to demonstrate this point. They presented a cat with
a series of clicks, and recorded the amplitude of the click-triggered
responses from the cochlear nucleus. When they showed the cat a

mouse, the amplitude of these responses was sharply reduced; it was as if the clicks were being "filtered out." The experiment has been widely cited, but it turns out not to be replicable; cats in other laboratories don't do this. The phenomenon was due to some sort of artifact. More recent work by Picton and Hillgard(1971) and their group at San Diego has shown that the opposite is true. There is no diminution in the activity of the cochlear nucleus when an individual (human or feline) stops paying attention to the auditory input of that ear. There are changes in overall neural activity, of course, but there is no "gate" at the periphery.

In my view (which is not very influential among neuropsychologists) there was never any chance of finding those peripheral filters. Attention is not like that. It would make no sense to close gates on any source of information; animals should always pick up all the information they can get. Mice might make noise, after all. As I have argued in various places (e.g. Neisser, 1976), attention is a matter of positive, constructive selection, not of negative exclusion. But what can a neuropsychologist do except look for the kinds of things that the prevailing psychological theory suggests?

RIEBER: We need a neurologist who is trained in psychology, or vice versa.

NEISSER: It's true that sometimes neurologists can stumble onto something of psychological interest without much benefit of theory. The work on motion detectors in the visual system is an example. Even there, however, the original discovery was motivated by ideas from outside neurophysiology itself. In their seminal paper on motion detectors in the frog, Lettvin and his collaborators (1959) give credit to Oliver Selfridge, a computer scientist, for the theoretical notions that stimulated their work. And although Selfridge's ideas were extremely ingenious, they did not really add up to a full psychological theory of motion perception. Possibly as a result, the work on neural detectors is still difficult to fit together with what we know about movement perception psychologically.

RIEBER: There is another idea I would like your reaction to. I have a hunch that there is a neobehaviorism developing. You can't kill off an old soldier easily, and there are many behaviorists around. They will just retool and come back with their own stuff, but in a different way. A lot of people are looking for a new paradigm; cognitive and especially developmental psychologists are taking advantage of the fact that behaviorism has been pushed out, but we are going to have some kind of neobehaviorism. It hasn't quite emerged yet, but I think it will.

NEISSER: Actually, we don't even need a neobehaviorism. There is still quite a lot of paleobehaviorism around. In many universities and institutions in America, "Psychology" is still pretty much limited to operant conditioning and behavior therapy.

RIEBER: What is your guess about the future?

NEISSER: It's hard to maintain a sustained theoretical commitment to the interaction between the organism and the environment,
because that interaction is so hard to study. You come up with a lot
of unique cases, of this person in this situation, from which it's
hard to generalize. It's even harder if the interaction develops
over time. Such situations are difficult to investigate scientifi-
cally, and don't produce quick results. Therefore there is always
a temptation to slip off into either a sheer environmentalism and
behaviorism on the one hand or a sheer rationalism and geneticism on
the other. I expect that we will go on seeing simplistic solutions
of one or the other kind, and some oscillation between them.

To make progress, we will have to look at that sustained interaction. There isn't any other satisfactory way. We can only hope
that we will gradually get better ideas of how to conceptualize and
describe it; to understand both what the person brings to the situation and what he finds in it. Progress will be slow, but we are
living at a time when new sources of information are opening up:
developmental studies and cross-cultural studies and animal studies
are giving us a lot of new ideas. It will be a long time before we
have synthesized them into an adequate conception of human nature.

RIEBER: Are they really new ideas, or are we just rediscovering
old ideas and perhaps putting them to a better test?

NEISSER: There will be a degree to which they seem familiar,
and someone will claim to have had them before, but they will be new
nevertheless. That's what the history of science suggests. There
are those who claim that modern atomic theory was not new in physics
because Democritus had an atomic theory in ancient Greece, but he
wouldn't have recognized the contemporary version.

Here's a better example, involving data. When Darwin sailed
around the world in the Beagle, he saw a profusion of new species and
environments that no naturalist had ever seen before. They were
crucial for his thinking. He probably could not have formulated the
theory of evolution if he had not had those experiences. All the
same, it can be argued that the theory of evolution was not entirely
new.

RIEBER: His grandfather Erasmus Darwin had it.

NEISSER: In a sense he did. Nevertheless, what we now know
about evolution would not have been recognized as familiar by Darwin's
grandfather. The history of science is full of cases where an old
idea becomes new because you see it in a new domain, and see new ways
of using it. So I am very hopeful that the information we are accumu-
lating will bring important new ways of thinking along with it. It

will be a long time, though, before a genuinely interactive theory
that captures a large share of the truth about human nature will be
generally accepted.

DIALOGUE V

Marcel Kinsbourne's Views on the Psychology of Language and Thought

Dr. Kinsbourne received his medical training at Oxford University and Guy's Hospital in London and specialized in prediatric neurology. He began an intensive program of neuropsychological research some twenty years ago. He was appointed University Lecturer in Psychology at Oxford in 1964, and Associate Professor in Pediatrics and Neurology at Duke University in 1967. In 1974 he moved to Canada where he was Professor of Pediatrics (Neurology) and Professor of Psychology till 1981. He is now Director of Behavioral Neurology at the Eunice Kennedy Shriver Center in Boston.

Dr. Kinsbourne's research centers on cognitive processes, their development, and their brain bases, and his studies range from infancy through childhood to the other end of the life span. They involve, in addition to normal people, children with developmental disabilities and adults with focal brain damage. His recent publications include an edited volume entitled "The Asymmetrical Function of the Brain," and "Children's Learning and Attention Problems" of which he is the senior author. In all, he has published some 200 scientific papers.

Dialogue V. Marcel Kinsbourne's Views on the Psychology of Language and Thought

I. What role does cognition play in the acquisition and the development of language? Do linguistic factors influence general cognitive development?

KINSBOURNE: Cognition is an essential prerequisite for the development of linguistic reference, but not of phonology. Phonological development is innately programmed and takes its initial course without reference to the environment. Babbling displays the phonological repertoire and babbling develops even in a profoundly deaf child who hears no sounds on which he can model his own utterances. When the individual hears normally, then over time his babble speech sounds will take on the patterns of the ambient verbalization, at which time they would assume the phonological characteristics of the particular language spoken, and soon after that the child will speak in words. The process of mapping these words onto the external reality, the acquisition of verbal reference, is another matter. This depends totally on cognitive development, specifically development of perception and of the ability to implement and perceive one's own actions.

RIEBER: Would you illustrate this with the example of perhaps how it relates to nominalization?

KINSBOURNE: When the child first utters the names of objects, he does so not in a movement vacuum, but in relationship to certain positional rearrangements of the whole body. I think these may have evolved from what in infants is called the tonic neck response. This is a positional adjustment in which the child turns his head and gazes toward the same location, extends the leg on the other side as if to swivel on while his opposite arm and same-sided leg are

145

flexed. The child is selectively orienting towards a location in
space and placing himself as if intending to walk toward it. Of
course, the child at the age at which the tonic neck reflex is most
prominent is far too young to be able actually to pursue the approach
sequence to the point of walking over to the object of attention.
Nevertheless, this selective orienting position is the building stone
on which the later perfected approach sequence are based. Now, it
is in the nature of a synergism such as the tonic neck response that
all the various rearrangements tend to occur together. Later in the
first year, movement and vocalization occur synergically. The baby
babbles while looking and pointing and when he begins to name, he
names the object at which he is looking and pointing. At that stage
the naming is part of the orienting synergism and cannot be dis-
sociated from it. It takes further mental maturation for the naming
to be possible without any sign of concurrent orienting towards the
named object. With further maturation even the naming itself can
become covert, that is, represented only in inner speech. So, naming
arises in the context of orientation. Incidentally, young babies
orient more often to the right than to the left. This may be why the
motor control mechanism for naming is on the same side of the brain
as the motor control mechanism for orienting to the right, namely the
left cerebral hemisphere. It is not in some lefthanded people. Also,
we have found that the children of non-righthanded parents do not
exhibit rightward bias of turning as infants. Similarly, when the
child learns words, he uses them initially in the context of experiencing or performing the actions described (or recollecting them in
their previous physical location). Subsequent development of the
ability to utter word sequences or phrases still reflects the mapping
of words on external reality, at least in the young child. Thus,
the young child is constrained to describe actions in the sequence
in which they appear to him to occur (agent-action-object) and other
syntactic arrangements are much later to develop. When he speaks
using this word order, one cannot assume that he has acquired a
linguistic rule. If the child is to use some form such as the passive
which infringes the experienced sequence of the action described,
then he has to abstract the words from their referents for purposes
of the mental manipulation in conforming with a linguistic rule that
he now has acquired, and that necessitates a relatively high level
of mental maturation. Before that stage he will systematically
misconstrue heard sentences which violate the customary relationship
of the referents. Disregarding the syntax, he will interpret the
sentence in a manner consistent with the way in which the referents
usually behave. It is in general only beyond the age of 5 that children are able to map words upon words (mentally manipulate verbal
forms as opposed to merely slavishly mapping them on events). Whereas
even before that age words are useful as economical codes by which
to remember, perhaps only beyond that stage do they become useful
instruments for problem-solving in that they are freed for purposes
of mental manipulation.

In reviewing what has been said, we notice one general phenomenon. This is that infants and children act out sequences of behavior which do not appear to achieve any immediate adaptive purpose, but are of a form which later will be put to adaptive use. Thus, babbling in itself does not necessarily achieve anything for the child, but later when the child recombines the babbled sounds into words, he can achieve certain goals by using more words. Rearranging the body so as to be in position to move towards an attended object serves the infant no purpose as it cannot walk. But later on that rearrangement will be the point of departure for locomotion. This type of anticipation of the content of behavior by its earlier appearing form characterizes children's play in general.

RIEBER: What makes you think that?

KINSBOURNE: When children play, they are not doing it for practice. What they do is often immediately within their powers, and far from them ceasing to do it, they keep doing it for a long time without getting any better at it. They move to a more complex level of behavior, not when they have learned the previous one, but when their brain is sufficiently mature for them to progress to that next level. It follows that acting out the behavioral potential at a particular level is not essential for progressing to the next level of behavioral potential. This can be inferred from empirical evidence. One instance is the child born without hands or feet, the so-called thalidomide baby who, nevertheless, develops normally as regards cognition. Another is the child who, on account of a congenital dislocation of the hips, is immobilized for the best part of his first year of life. On being released from splints and plasters, he shows no need to first catch up on and act out the various activities that he would have performed had he been free to do so during his period of immobility. It becomes clear that theories which attribute developmental disabilities to failure to act out a particular level of motor development cannot be correct and remedial methods based on them are therefore irrational. It is the sequence of brain maturation, generating evermore sophisticated behavioral potential that matters, not whether at any particular point the potential was fully realized in action or not. The act of communication itself gradually is carried out by enlisting component behaviors, such as pointing, which originally are used in "orienting-for-self" and only later to "point-out" (orient-for-another). Similarly, the earlier words may not be communicative in content, but only be used in a communicative context and in concert with the other communicative behaviors several months later.

RIEBER: So if children don't play for practice, why do they play?

KINSBOURNE: I don't know for sure, but here is a guess. For each one of us there is some level of enjoyment with an environment

that keeps us pleasantly occupied. If too little is going on, we
feel restless. If too much is happening, we feel overloaded. If we
can respond in some pertinent fashion to what is happening, we
discharge that feeling of overloaded. If we are precluded from doing
this, we feel thwarted, and discharge our impulse to action by going
into some rhythmic action routine, like drumming our fingers or
twitching, or even, in extremes, whirling, spinning, flapping or head
banging. So, given a structured environment, it helps us feel good
to do something with it, regardless of whether what we do serves some
adaptive purpose external to the activity itself. Children play not
to achieve a goal or to get better at some performance. They play
because it helps them feel good. At the level of the brain, playing
discharges excess activation in some homeostatic system, bringing it
down to an acceptable level.

RIEBER: So this would apply to babbling also, wouldn't it?
We know that children babble without necessarily monitoring the sounds
they make by ear as deaf children babble as much initially as normal
children. This would support your hypothesis that they do so under
control of some preprogrammed homeostatic mechanism in the brain.

KINSBOURNE: Right. So the brain maturation generates the
potential, the environment generates the opportunity for its realization and the child's motivational characteristics will determine
whether he takes advantage of his brain maturation and environmental
opportunities. A further implication is that impediments in motor
performance would not be expected to impede cognitive development in
general, nor even the internal representation of motor performance
in particular. An instance is the famous Lenneberg case of a child
who acquired language comprehension in a normal fashion although
totally unable to utter. The case of stuttering can also be considered in this light. The stutterer's articulatory defect does not
appear to detract from his ability to construct internalized verbal
representation, in other words, inner speech. Of course, with all
stutterers there are circumstances under which they do not stutter.
At those times they realize their potential for completely normal
speech expression. At any rate, even with respect to the particular
combinations of speech sounds that elicit their stutter, their speech
development is not compromised. Some stutters do have delayed
language development. This is a separate outcome of a common cause;
an antecedent factor that caused stuttering on the one hand and
delayed language development on the other. The situation is similar
to that in lefthandedness. Lefthandedness is mostly related to
completely normal cognitive development, but in some instances it is
related to developmental disability. It occurs in the normal person
in the general population, and that is the consequence of genetic
diversity. Where it occurs in, say, a severely retarded person, it
could be a separate consequence of the severe brain damage that also
caused the retardation. The damage changed a genotypic dextral into
a phenotypic sinistral.

Language is one of the available forms of overt and covert representation of reality. It happens to be very convenient and efficient for organisms capable of programming very rapid transitions from speech sound to speech sound, as we humans are (by virtue of our left hemispheric sequencing ability). But this is by no means the only way in which external reality can be represented and mentally manipulated. One might quite effectively design some other representational system, for instance, in a relational "right hemispheric" mode, within the sensory-motor capabilities of a nonhuman animal, and demonstrate that animal could use that system in internalized fashion for purposes of planning. This attitude views human language in the context of biological continuity.

RIEBER: What is your position regarding whether linguistic factors influence cognitive development?

KINSBOURNE: This can be answered either in a trivial fashion or in so general a way that the proposition becomes untestable. If we confine ourselves to the usual level of discourse about Whorf's hypothesis and instance the fact that Eskimos use many different words to designate different states of texture and consistency of snow, unlike people who live in climates where this information is not essential, then it can be easily demonstrated that anybody can learn those separate verbal references once they have focused their selective attention on perceptual distinctions which the Eskimos find worth noting whereas we mostly do not. Nor is an experiment such as Lenneberg's on our better ability to recognize those colors for which we have verbal labels than colors for which we have none, a valid test of Whorf's hypothesis. Rather, Whorf's proposition deals with language systems that are so different that the manner the person mentally represents reality is different depending on the language in which he was raised. The Hopi Indian who might use adjectives such as shining, flowing, slashing, rushing to designate what we name "waterfall" would, according to Whorf, mentally represent a waterfall in quite a different fashion and in that way experience reality and its rearranged possibilities differently from ourselves. The problem with this strong proposition is that it is essentially untestable. To design a valid test an experimenter would have to bridge that conceptual gap and deal with reality from the perspectives of the users of each of the two different languages. Now, if he could do that, then Whorf's logic would automatically become inapplicable to that particular instance and the experimental test is disqualified. As a psychologist, I therefore confine myself to pointing out that the vocabulary we use and the phraseology to which we are accustomed certainly constrain our habitual patterns of thought. Words focus our attention on those aspects of the environment to which they refer. If an environmental feature can be labeled verbally, that helps make it more salient and more likely to attract attention. However, this is not of fundamental interest because suitable experience or training could overcome individual differences in this respect. Whorf's

hypothesis, properly understood, is an issue for philosophers rather
than psychologists to resolve.

II. *How is the acquisition and development of language influenced
     by interpersonal and intrapersonal verbal and nonverbal
     behavior?*

KINSBOURNE: Let's begin with the issue of critical periods for
language learning. The literature gives no definite support to the
notion that a critical period exists in humans subsequent to which
the individual's brain becomes incapable of acquiring language at
all or language at more than a rudimentary level. It is true that
some children deprived of early language experience have shown less
than the normally expected rate of language acquisition once that
experience was supplied. But there are two confounded factors in
these studies. One is that when dealing with a single individual
one cannot be sure retrospectively that his language potential was
normal in the first place. The other is that the circumstances under
which human beings could conceivably be deprived of language experience for a number of years are so grossly abnormal (presumably
associated with psychopathology on the part of significant others)
that the child's own emotional development can't help but be significantly or even severely affected. This will reflect upon the child's
motivational state for learning language when he is finally given
the opportunity. It is unclear to what extent cognitive and to what
extent emotional factors interfere when children who were deprived
of language for periods of years are finally given a language experience.

RIEBER: Yes indeed. In fact this is true in the case of Itard's
Wild Boy as well.

KINSBOURNE: None of this, of course, contradicts the clearly
established fact that the plasticity of the nervous system decreases
in animals as well as humans over time. It is just that language
learning is not an instance that clearly illustrates that principle.
Take, for instance, the case of second language. Others have made
much of the supposed fact that older children and adults have remarkable trouble in learning a second language. It is really only with
respect to phonology rather than the other levels of language behavior
that this case can at all plausibly be argued. But there again we
have a serious confound. The person who learns a second language
late rather than early in life has "overlearned" the first language.
In other words, he has learned to the point of extreme fluency or
automaticity a set of responses from which he is now supposed to
deviate when speaking the second language. However, he is in no
position simply to suppress the early learned set of responses completely, even if he could, because typically he doesn't stop using
the first language completely, but rather, as a bilingual person,
uses both. Thus, he is in a state of severe response competition,

the more overlearned responses being hard to suppress completely.
Nor is he necessarily motivated to make that effort, as he can make
himself understood anyway. The young child who learns in parallel
responses from both languages would not be in such a response conflict. Indeed, he might well be in a favorable position for learning
to speak yet another language using correct phonology. This issue
has to do not with neuronal plasticity, but rather with mechanisms
of learning. Certainly, it would be useful to know what would happen
to second language learning under circumstances where the learner of
a second language completely relinquishes the use of the first. (This
would be particularly interesting if it happened during the adult
years).

    RIEBER: It would be most profitable to have the data from such
a study, but, alas, I am not aware of the existence of such in the
literature.

    KINSBOURNE: There is another fallacy in relating the young
child's supposedly great ability to learn a second language to neurological plasticity. There is a subtle logical discontinuity here.
Plasticity is usually discussed in terms of the ability of the nervous
system to compensate for damage by shifting the location of control
of the affected behavior. Plasticity is the ability of the central
nervous system to reorganize its functions and to compensate for loss
of part of that system so as still to supply the relevant operation.
There is no evidence that plasticity in this sense has anything to
do with learning ability. The idea that the younger the child, the
more receptive he is to learning not only lacks an empirical basis,
but also has nothing to do with plasticity in the neurobiological
sense.

    RIEBER: When events are experienced, is the brain itself changed
because of the experience?

    KINSBOURNE: Any experienced event potentially changes the brain.
We have a repertoire of possible behaviors and we have a system for
selecting among them depending on the contingencies of the moment.
Learning consists of gradually making certain responses more probable
and others less probable in particular contexts. So, what happens
with experience is that we react with higher probability (and shorter
latency and more automatically) in certain fashions when the situation
is sufficiently familiar (that is, capable of being related to previous experiences). Someone who has learned something in this sense
cannot easily unlearn even if he wants to because it is now part of
his response repertoire. In that sense his brain has changed. It
would take even greater a period of contrary practice to dismiss the
consequences of that learning. So in that sense all experiences to
a greater or lesser degree, depending on their nature and relevance,
can change the way the nervous system is organized as manifested by
the way it subsequently controls behavior.

RIEBER: Does that imply that the infant is born tabula-rasa as it were?

KINSBOURNE: No. I am not proposing that the newborn infant is a tabula-rasa of equiprobable response. I already pointed out that the infant is neuronally prewired for certain patterns of responding. He responds primarily to color and secondarily to form and normally not at all to orientation or sequence. Color and form are high on the "perceptual hierarchy." If one attenuates the salient perceptual attributes or if the infant becomes able to habituate to them (and thereby render them less salient than other coexisting attributes) then he does become capable of responding to dimension lower on the perceptual hierarchy, like orientation or sequence. As the brain becomes more mature, the person becomes more readily able to move down the perceptual hierarchy by detaching his attention from more salient to less salient attributes (the process that Piaget called decentration). So, whereas the infant's response capabilities are constrained by an innate hierarchy of salience, the mature individual can learn to overcome the innately formed response tendencies and to respond with high probability to certain arbitrary conjunctions of stimuli with arbitrary response patterns. When we move our fingers we find certain sequences easier to perform than others because the motor control center in the brain is prewired in that fashion. The concert pianist learns to overcome those innate arrangements and acquire tremendous control over the sequences of finger movements that he can implement. It indicated the power of the biological pre-programming how much and how continually the pianist has to practice to overcome these preprogrammed constraints. No peripheral influences can change the brain's structure. But they do change priorities among the possible behaviors that the brain can implement.

III. Are the verbal and nonverbal signal systems interrelated?

KINSBOURNE: There are several nonverbal signalling systems. We will consider three.

The flow of speech is modified by changes in rate and rhythm, pauses, and contrastive stress. These prosodic attributes certainly convey and enrich meaning. A dramatic illustration is to be found in acute jargon aphasia. The patient, once addressed, responds with a continual and protracted flow of unintelligible phonation. The speech sounds proper convey no meaning. However, prosody is preserved, in isolation, and much that is idiosyncratic to the speaker, typical of his ethnic and social group, and indicative of his affect, is preserved. So, neuropsychologically, the verbal and prosodic aspects of speech are separable. Therefore, they must be represented differently in the brain. But they are of course intimately linked.

Speech is usually accompanied by facial, gestural and even whole body expression. Such expression, though usually coordinated with

speech is separable from it, and can be inhibited voluntarily or
through habit in cultural groups that disapprove of communication
that takes this form. Usually, these acts are involuntary. Some of
the gestures represent the verbal message itself in that they are
entrained in it, and punctuate it predictably, for instance at hesitation pauses. They represent, not so much the flow of words, as
the referents and concepts that are being expressed. They make
concrete the sweep of mental imagery that constitutes much of preverbal thought.

Then there are custom-made nonverbal signalling systems for use
by those who cannot use words with facility. The best developed of
these, American Sign Language, is thought to be a language in its own
right. It can be used in parallel with words, but appears to be
represented elsewhere in the brain. This could be because it capi-
talized on distinctions in visuospatial patterning rather than
auditory transitions. Commonality in localization in the brain is
determined not by uniformity of purpose ("communication") but congruence of means. Different parts of the brain lend themselves to
different _means_ for communicating.

IV. *How can one best deal with the issue of nature versus nurture
     in our attempts to unravel the basic issues in the field of
     language and cognition?*

     (a) *Of what importance is the biological basis of language
         perception and production?*

     (b) *Of what importance is the study of individuals who suffer
         from pathological conditions of language and thought?*

KINSBOURNE: Innate preprogramming provides a set of available
responses the probabilities of which are intensely biased with respect
to the particular contingencies that will favor release any one of
them. The environment then provides adaptive cause for modifying
that initial predisposition depending on the particular circumstances.
The more instructive the environment is, the better one is able to
modify one's response probabilities accordingly. What is an intelligent person? A person who is particularly well able to respond in
improbable fashion when such response best meets the existing adaptive
need. Given a problem that has an obvious solution, he need not be
intelligent to try out that obvious possibility. If, however, his
attempt doesn't work (i.e. the problem is a difficult one), the more
intelligent person will shift to the next most salient hypothesis
and therefore make the next most probable response. As he continues
to fail to achieve his goal, he will shift down the hierarchy of
probable hypotheses and use less and less probable responses to the
point that he will respond in fashions that appear to be actually
contradicted by public experience (like Einstein's proposition that
light can bend). The ability to entertain improbabilities, and to

depart from the most familiar response or from attending to the most salient aspect of the situation, is intelligent behavior.

As linguistic behavior is just one aspect of cognitive behavior, the foregoing applies to language. Verbal proficiency is exemplified by the ability to use words in improbable combinations when these improbable combinations happen better to specify or represent the thought called for that particular purpose. We are here basically discussing the nuance. The person with better verbal skills is able to deploy lower frequency terminology when this better characterizes what he wants to communicate.

RIEBER: How would you approach this problem?

KINSBOURNE: There are several ways of addressing this question. One might ask, of what importance is the fact that the human brain is preprogrammed for the utterance of speech sounds? It is, of course, crucially important for developing linguistic capability mediated by the spoken word. One might ask, of what importance are individual differences in the preprogramming? One can ask this question in two different ways: about individual differences in the degree of sophistication of the verbal facility wherever it is in the brain, or about the particular localization of that facility within the brain. These are very different questions.

The individual with a superior linguistic facility must possess a more sophisticated neural substrate to enable to do this. We don't know the characteristics of such neuronal sophistication but may speculate. Are the neurons more or less (more differentially) interconnected? I suspect that as the control system in the brain becomes more differentiated, neurons lose connections rather than gain them.

In evolutionary perspective, the more primitive the nervous system the more interconnected it is. Invertebrates have nerve nets. Vertebrates differ from invertebrates in that their neurons are less interconnected than is the case in a nerve net. Every neuron does not need to communicate directly with all the rest. Our brains are large because we need differential distance between neurons. In order to permit neurons to interconnect with different degrees of closeness, rather than all interconnect virtually to the same extent, our brains have to be rich in neurons. It is by the intercalation of additional neurons to implement this differential connectivity that what I call functional cerebral space has to be so greatly expanded. The consequences of differential location of control mechanism in functional cerebral space I will come to later. Without such differential connectivity, we would be limited to mass response to mass stimulation and could not, as we do, finely tune our behavior to the needs of the moment, that represent the intersect of many perceptual memorial and motivational parameters. So as the brain becomes more intricate during phylogeny (and possibly even during

ontogeny) there is a loss of neuronal connection (or inhibition at
the synapses connecting many of the neurons, which would have a
similar effect functionally). Neuronal organization becomes more
heterogenous.

From an evolutionary perspective we might argue that when a
particular facility is used with increasing specificity, then it
becomes less interconnected, that is, further removed in functional
distance from most of the rest of the brain. In animals that use
the forepaws and hindpaws in concert for postural control and for
crude grasp, there is heavy interconnection between the corresponding
primary sensory-motor areas across the callosal interconnection
between the two halves of the brain. In humans the sensory-motor
control of the fingers of the hand is isolated on each side whereas
control centers for the axial (proximal and truncal musculature)
remain interconnected. This is because in humans the fingers are no
longer involved in postural control and grasp is usually not bimanual.
They therefore may be partly released from direct influence by the
various parts of the body that respond to environment changes by
changing general bodily positions. Instead they come under the more
specific control of that part of the motor cortex which programs them
in their highly differentiated and individual behavior.

The behavioral counterpart is instructive. For instance, one
becomes gradually able to wiggle one finger separately from the other
after the first year of his life. We do this not according to a keyboard principle, triggering the control center of one finger, leaving
the others unchanged in their activation level. Rather, we program
all four fingers to wiggle but at the same time stop the wiggling of
three of them by downstream inhibition. It is rather like hitting
all four notes of a keyboard chord but having the effects of three
of these contacts blocked downstream. An analogous principle applies
to the verbal behavior of some early language learners. Such children
acquire certain stereotypic labels and phrases and initially utter
them all of a piece. With increasing verbal sophistication they are
able to utter components while suppressing the rest of the phrase.
Ultimately, they are able to combine components from different phrases
into new combinations. But even in the mature adult time constraints
or stress will reveal the tendency to respond preferentially according
to these primitive patterns. This issue leads into the question about
the potential fruitfulness of the studying of abnormal behavior in
order to learn more about the normal.

Many normal young children echo words, and thus echolalia represents the necessarily holistic manner in which young children who
pick up phrases do so before they are able to analyse them into their
components. The persistence and greater prevalence of echolalia
among autistic children results from their inability to map their
phonological system on to their cognitive system. This leaves their
words and phrases deprived of reference. There is then no obvious

reason why they should break them up into components and recombine them, as the lack of reference disconnects the verbal behavior from the contingencies that normally control the development of children's word usage. The notorious formality of the speech of autists reflects the same lack of flexibility in modifying heard phraseology for adaptive purposes. These children sometimes exhibit quite high levels of development of nonverbal abilities, but their language, which may be phonologically relatively advanced, seems not to be used to represent what they are doing or what is happening around them. It is not put to referential use. Instead, they often use people instrumentally, steering and manipulating them toward satisfying their needs in ways that avoid the use of language. Autistic language perhaps can be a living instance of the "free floating phonology," that I referred to earlier, and illustrates the extent to which the speech system may develop independently of any cognitive basis. This would account for the common observation that many such children, when tested on vocabulary tests, seem to be very restricted in their vocabularies (if they speak at all) but that if an inventory is kept of their occasional utterances over time their vocabulary is found to be reasonably rich. The reason, of course, is that if a person uses words nonreferentially, it is hard to predict when he will use a particular word, and therefore hard to arrange to be present at a time when he might use it. The test situation might be the wrong time. A special instance of this dissociation between phonology and cognition has to do with personal reference. Autistic children often fail to use the first personal pronoun. One should not conclude that they lack a sense of self. Even if they have subjectivity, a mental representation of themselves as entities with continuity in space and time, they have not mapped the first personal pronoun on to this construct.

We can now address the distinction between how a particular neuronal system that controls an aspect of behavior develops, and where in the brain it is located. The extravagant claims for cognitive differences based on localization and specifically lateralization differences appear to be without substance. An attribute may, in some individuals, deviate from the norm either on account of inferior genetic programming brain damage or the like, or because it is of little adaptive relevance, so that variability is tolerated by natural selective processes. I suspect that with regard to the anomalous cerebral organization of some lefthanders, the latter is the case. Whereas righthanders are left lateralized for language in almost every case, lefthanders may be the same, the opposite or bilateralized. Nobody has succeeded in showing any convincing difference in efficiency in the various cognitive modes or in cognitive style (that is, choice between such modes in particular situtations), depending on lateralization pattern, there is coexisting brain damage. Then the brain damage itself could have caused both the behavioral anomaly and the lefthandedness. If there are functional consequences of differential localization between ostensibly normal individuals

and the general population the right experiment to demonstrate these
have not yet been done. But why then is function localized? Why
are not all functions represented everywhere? This is an important
question because, after all, in some people it does seem that function
is spread more thin than in others. If there is an adaptive value
for localization, I suspect that this would only become apparent when
people perform more than one task at a time. In a typical psycho-
metric or experimental psychological task, the subject is asked to
do only one thing, and as far as we can tell, for such work it doesn't
matter how the brain is organized. It is when you give a person two
things to do at the same time, both of which demand his attention,
then the relationship between the centers in the brain that control
the two activities matters. The brain is a highly linked neural net-
work, which acts as a functional cerebral space. I hypothesize that
any locus of activation within that space potentially spreads its
particular pattern of activation throughout the space, but mostly to
the most connected loci and least to those parts of the brain that
are further in functional distance (that is, least connected - for
instance, separated by the greatest number of synapses). Now, if you
want to perform a complex act that requires two different types of
programming which have to be run concurrently, then ideally the
control neurons should be as separated as possible so that it is
possible to interpose an inhibitory barrier which blocks cross-talk
between them and therefore interferences in the efficient workings
of both. Perhaps their identifying abilities are left lateralized
and relational ones right lateralized not because these are alternative modes of thinking between which we have to choose, but on the
contrary, because they are integrated modes of thinking both of which
we use most of the time in combination. If relational (analogue) and
itemizing (digital) programs run at the same time, they should not
interfere with each other so that their products can be exactly to
specification when they come to be integrated into the final act.
It would make adaptive sense, then, for them to be lateralized in
opposite hemispheres. This explains why areas that usually function
in concert such as hearing and speech are more closely interconnected
than areas which do not. The main reason is not that this helps set
up more efficient communication channels to send information from
one area to the other sequentially, but that in behavior both activities function in parallel. Because their function is guided by the
same superordinate principle, it can be easily and efficiently integrated because they are adjacent in functional cerebral space.
Again, it makes sense for speech and right hand control to be adjacent
and highly interconnected because for speaking and writing you may
use the same superordinate program, tranducing it into vocal or manual
action, or both.

The critical test for lefthanders who are ill-lateralized would
be to give them unrelated activities to do concurrently and see if
there is more interference than in righthanders in whom the relevant
control centers are further apart. This prediction was supported in
the one such study reported so far.

RIEBER: What are the implications of this approach?

KINSBOURNE: One implication of the functional cerebral distance model is that when two processes have to be carried out at the same time, it is useful for one of them to be fully automatized and therefore minimally requiring of attention whereupon the other one could have benefit of the full power of conscious effort and the full extent of functional cerebral space. Speaking conversationally is an instance. When you speak you say what you have already thought and while you are saying it, you are thinking about the next thing about which you will then speak. For the fluent speaker, speaking is highly automatized, and does not interfere with the concurrent pre-thinking of the next proposition. The hesitation pause is not due to some limitation in the ability to speak, but is because the thought that is about to be expressed has not been formulated sufficiently explicitly to permit further words to be uttered right away.

Whereas speaking out loud communicates your thoughts, speaking covertly to oneself encodes them for better remembering. But formulating one's thoughts in words lightens the load on immediate memory. This is important because effective thinking requires the constructive combination of multiple items and it is not possible to combine items unless one has them already accessible in mind at the same time. Recoding these concepts into words is economical of functional cerebral space, in which they have simultaneously to be told, and renders them more accessible for purposes of the overall thought process.

RIEBER: Can you give us an illustration of this?

KINSBOURNE: Yes! As a teenager I was often aware of having multiple incipient thoughts at the same time. I remember walking over a familiar open space knowing that I had four or five thoughts that were original in mind, and afraid of losing and not recovering one or more of these. I would then, if possible, verbalize each in turn holding the others in some preverbal store and hoping that none of them would slip away before I had perpetuated them in words. Once verbalized, I knew I could recover the thought at will. Occasionally I would be conscious of having lost a thought because I had spent too much time verbalizing the others and consequently had a sense of intense frustration and personal loss. I had no way of knowing whether this thought would ever come back.

RIEBER: Does the study of aphasia provide us with anything relevant here?

KINSBOURNE: Yes! The study of aphasia is potentially relevant to normal language. Lashley told us that focal brain damage affords us a biological factor analysis. What are the components of language behavior? When a focal lesion within the language territory deprives

people of the ability to perform certain language acts, but leaves
other intact, this is direct evidence that a particular component
was selectively eliminated. But if every time a focal lesion prejudices function a, function b is also lost, the probability increases
that these functions are both subserved by the same brain territory
and perhaps are different expressions of the same basic mechanism.
This is important in the simulation of behavior, if the simulator
wishes to simulate the real brain rather than some conceptual system
which coincides with the brain only in producing comparable outputs.
Failing such a biological anchor one comes up with formal systems
of analysis which may relate to man-made categories, but have no
biological reality. The currently fashionable digital computer
simulation of behavior must be appraised with the realization that
the computer may simulate outcomes very accurately without in any way
resembling the brain in the way in which it achieves the endpoint,
but rather use totally different mechanisms. In fact, we know that
this is so. Consider the limited capacity of the human operator.
We know that people can do more than one thing at a time. But if
they do, then they don't do each of the two things as well as if they
were doing just one of them by itself. Computers can easily be so
designed as not to be limited in this fashion. This is a useful outcome in that it falsifies certain possible models of brain mechanisms.
If functional localization were complete and the brain consisted of
a number of completely independent channels, then this capacity
limitation would not be expected. Perhaps the reasons are the ones
I have already given. We may regard functional localization as
relative in the sense that a particular area is primarily in charge
of a particular form of behavior control, but when in action its
pattern of activity spreads, and when it is inactivated other parts
are often able to compensate to a greater or a lesser degree. This
relates to the earlier proposition that development begins in terms
of unified wholes and maturation brings differentiation. A mechanical
device may be limited in capacity because it has a limited source of
energy. Some psychologists have suggested that such resource limitations account for human capacity limitations. But as I have
explained, these limitations are inevitable in the case of the brain
because, being a highly linked system, we can see how two concurrent
cerebrally controlled activities would interfere and limit each
other's efficiency. We need not postulate additional explanations
for that limitation.

The study of aphasia can give some basic insights into language
as opposed to communication mechanisms. When a person is aphasic,
has he lost the ability to communicate verbally or has he lost the
ability to communicate in any form whatever? Is it a problem of
verbal signalling or a more broadly defined problem of symbolic
behavior? This can be tested by determining what a person with global
aphasia can still learn to do in order to communicate. Can he use
morse code, semaphore, sign language and so forth? We find that meta-
languages such as writing and morse code are indeed lost, but that

sign and gestural language as forms of expression are maintained.
This teaches us that communicative systems are not all represented
in the same place, but rather that verbal communication and gestural
communication are differently represented. This theoretical insight
also offers practical opportunity. Patients with aphasia or with
developmental language disorders including autism who presumably have
intact right hemisphere abilities can perhaps be taught to communicate
by sign languages which permit a mapping of that code directly onto
perceived events (whereas the verbal facility may be destroyed or
may be disconnected). There are reports of the rehabilitation of
aphasic and autistic individuals that suggest this might work.

Within aphasia there are separate syndromes which again tell us
something about the components of the language system. It is clear
that lesions may differentially prejudice verbal expression and verbal
comprehension, and this is relevant to theories of the neurological
basis of language. Again, within part-syndromes of receptive aphasia
there is the condution variant in which repetition is more difficult
than comprehension and the transcallosal variant in which the reverse
is the case. Again, at some point in the information flow, comprehension and repetition must be separately represented. As we improve
our taxonomy of the aphasias, we will know more about the components
of normal language mechanisms.

RIEBER: Of what relevance is the language of the psychotic in
this context?

KINSBOURNE: Psychotic language illustrates quite a different
point, namely, how language maps upon cognition. Psychotic language
is hard to identify with or comprehend because it represents a
personal frame of reference which is idiosyncratic. The linguistic
development of the profoundly deaf can reveal the extent to which
verbal mediation is necessary for intellectual development. In other
words, identify those not necessarily overtly verbal processes which
utilize verbal mediation and therefore would only with great difficulty be acquired by people who are unable to deploy that type of
mediation. A further distinction can be made with the help of those
who have a sign language at their disposal. Particularly if it turns
out to be correct that communication systems like American Sign
Language are right hemisphere mediated, it would be of interest to
determine what subset of a normal person's intellectual repertoire
can be supported by this alternate system of arbitrary encoding of
information. Incidentally, the issue is not whether deaf people in
general do as well as normal controls on a variety of tasks. The
issue is how well a deaf person can do although he is deaf. So if
some deaf people achieve normal intelligence in a major sphere of
cognition, the fact that others don't is of lesser importance as those
others may have fallen short for nonspecific reasons like lessened
motivation, restricted opportunity or coincidental brain damage.

*V.   Of what importance is the current research in comparative
      psycholinguistics (recent attempts to train chimpanzees and/or
      apes via sign language or any other method)?*

KINSBOURNE: It is interesting to wonder to what extent the
training of apes in communications relies upon principles related to
those just discussed, say, with the deaf or the autistic. Apes do
not have the mechanical articulation skills to make it feasible to
train them to speak in human fashion. However, other forms of
communication have been imparted to them and there is some reason to
suppose that the ape can then use the system constructively rather
than purely in a slavish fashion. It would be more interesting still
to know whether the animal who has learned the code can use it to
enrich his ability to make plans and solve problems. This would be
an interesting, indirect but controlled way to test the relationship
between language and cognition.

Much has been made recently of the fact that whereas children
"pick up language spontaneously without specific instruction," apes
have to be trained laboriously over a long period of intensive
structured practice. This may have more to do with perceptual
salience than with any fundamental difference between the animal's
and the human being's ability to master a communication system.

RIEBER: What specifically do you mean by that?

KINSBOURNE: The fact that one can hear accurately sound coming
from any direction makes it unnecessary to develop the ability to
orient to sound specifically before being able to imitate or decode
it. This makes sound a particularly suitable vehicle for natural
language learning by infants (and also explains why they become able
to localize auditory later than visual stimuli). Visual communication
presupposes accurate selective orientation, and this is itself a
developmental issue.

Incidentally, it is a remarkable fact that apes, though they
selectively orient, do not point.

RIEBER: Why is that?

KINSBOURNE: I don't know. But if I am right about early speech
being synergically linked with pointing to infants, then here we have
a further difference between human and non-human primates relevant
to why the former develop language whereas the latter do not. It
would be interesting to find out whether in the time mock response
of apes there is, as in humans, extension of the ipsilateral arm,
and whether the mature animal can be taught to point.

It seems to me that psychology is at this time in what might
be called a pre-Darwinian phase, in a Linnean phase. It is faculty

psychology updated. Psychologists basically do what Wundt did.
They measure the limits of performance in increasingly sophisticated
ways. How much can be remembered? How quickly can something be
perceived? How many things can be retained at the same time? What
is the duration of the experiential present? The problem is that
anybody can choose to measure whatever they please and without any
particular reason Newell characterized this by saying "you can't play
Twenty Questions with nature and win." You may define a question and
answer it, but the answer does not necessarily have any generality
or illuminate anything beyond the phenomenon that is being studied.
My main reservation about contemporary experimental psychology is
that although it is very sophisticated methodologically, it is
essential atheoretical (beyond some primitive computer analyzing).
Now many insightful psychologists are aware of the fact that our
paradigms are very limited and they try to remedy this in one of three
ways. They try to design a very spare and fundamental paradigm which
they hope will have the generality that one looks for (such as Saul
Sternberg's memory scanning), look for some universal metric with
which one can measure a variety of different phenomena (such as bits
of information) or they seek to define invariants such as George
Miller's "magic number 7," or John Stroud's perceptual moment. The
paradigms are recalcitrantly limited, the "invariants" vary. We
have the geography of mental function. We know some heights, some
depths and some contours. But we have no unified concept which
explains why the heights are where they are and the depths where they
are. Now, I don't know what the unifying system will be when it
arrives, but I will make some comments on the possibilities.

Basic to mental functioning are its selective and constructive
aspects. Selection and construction are successively implemented
for any behavior, be it perception, problem solving, language or
performance. In each case the individual first selects what information to work with, putting himself into position to pick up that
information as a designated subset of the total ambient information.
Then, selectively attending to that subset he ascertains the actual
state of the relevant cues and constructs out of them a representation of the individual reality of the moment and compares that
reality to the state of affairs with respect to the goal he has in
mind. In other words, having extracted the right cues he blows them
up into a coherent picture of how they relate to each other at the
time and then reads off his experience what are his chances given
that present state of affairs of achieving the goal that he wishes
to achieve. He then determines how he might optimize those possibilities.

It is with respect to selection that cybernetic reasoning
particularly applies. Selection is programmed at the neural level
in terms of negative and positive feedback.

Negative feedback resolves opponent processes along the vector resultant of their interaction. Positive feedback resolves competition for control of an output mechanism. The more mature the nervous system, the more effectively the feedback system will proceed, the more finely is selection modulated, and the more decisively is competition resolved. I study this in terms of brain organization by simple models such as my functional cerebral space principle, and in this way illustrate how these balances work.

With respect to the constructive aspect, the representation of experienced reality, which occurs once one has made one's selection, this has to do with combinative intricacies of neuronal function about which we don't have any clue as yet. When someone discovers how to study this, they will be studying the cerebral states that represent the selected reality.

VI. *What are the most important and promising applications of research in the psychology of language and cognition?*

KINSBOURNE: The emerging paradigm will differ from existing ones not only in having much greater generality, but in addressing itself to the brain states that actually underlie cognition rather than merely dealing at the behavioral level (in psychology) or the brain level (in neurophysiology). It will be thought necessary to check the validity of hypotheses about mental phenomena with respect to brain function. It will not be regarded as sufficient to demonstrate that a model successfully simulates the actual behavior unless it can be also shown that simulation actually addresses the fashion in which the behavior is generated in human beings. Failing that, artificial intelligence is of limited interest biologically. Certainly one cannot assume that if the outcome is the same, then the manner in which it was achieved has something in common with the way the brain operates. Models of brain function can be tested with respect to abnormal brain states induced either by lesions or by psychopharmacological intervention. The model should predict the effects of manipulations of brain state and those predictions should be borne out if the model is to have any credibility. For instance, take a hypothesized personality variable such as introversion-extroversion or reflectivity-impulsivity. To see whether one or both of these have biological as opposed to merely conceptual reality. one can determine whether a person's position on this proposed dimension can be manipulated by changing the state of the brain, for instance by use of psycho-active drugs. We find that giving amphetamines shifts cognitive style towards the reflectivity end of one dimension, but has no significant effect on the other (extroversion-introversion) dimension. Thus, the dimension of impulsivity-reflectivity is shown to have biological reality whereas the other dimension is not yet shown to have such reality, at least through the outcome of this particular study. So when I show that the hyperactive child, who is pathologically impulsive, becomes less so

and more normal given a particular drug, I am discovering something
that transcends hyperactivity. I am showing that impulsivity is a
biologically valid dimension of individual variation.

RIEBER: Does this not stress the importance of individual
differences?

KINSBOURNE: Yes. Once we have a really useful model for
language and cognition, we will be able to make much more powerful
statements about individual differences. Insofar as psychology has
an applied purpose, that must deal with individual differences in one
form or another. So whereas basic psychology has models that strive
for species-specific overriding generality, the applications of these
models will serve to help us to find out how individuals differ.
One then will be able to classify individuals in terms of their
different intellectual potentials much more powerfully than is at
present possible.

Index